The Truth Will Make Us Free!

Jeffery Bishop

TEACH Services, Inc.
PUBLISHING
www.TEACHServices.com • (800) 367-1844

World rights reserved. This book or any portion thereof may not be copied or reproduced in any form or manner whatever, except as provided by law, without the written permission of the publisher, except by a reviewer who may quote brief passages in a review.

The author assumes full responsibility for the accuracy of all facts and quotations as cited in this book. The opinions expressed in this book are the author's personal views and interpretations, and do not necessarily reflect those of the publisher.

This book is provided with the understanding that the publisher is not engaged in giving spiritual, legal, medical, or other professional advice. If authoritative advice is needed, the reader should seek the counsel of a competent professional.

Copyright © 2023 Jeffery Bishop

Copyright © 2023 TEACH Services, Inc.

ISBN-13: 978-1-4796-1561-2 (Paperback)

ISBN-13: 978-1-4796-1562-9 (ePub)

Library of Congress Control Number: 2022922344

Unless otherwise indicated, all Scripture quotations are from the King James Version (KJV). Other versions used are:

The Bible In Basic English was printed in 1965 by Cambridge Press in England. It is published without any copyright notice in the public domain. (BBE)

Contemporary English Version. Copyright © 1995 by American Bible Society. Used by Permission. (CEV)

Scripture taken from the Good News Translation—Second Edition, Copyright © 1992 by American Bible Society. Used by Permission. (GNT)

Table of Contents

Chapter 1. The Truth about the Little Horn Power 7

Chapter 2. The Council of Trent 24

Chapter 3. Sabbath or Sunday? 27

Chapter 4. The Sabbath, Is It for Jews or for Gentiles? 34

Chapter 5. A Significant Catholic Document 44

Chapter 6. What is the "Truth" about the Mark of the Beast? 53

Chapter 7. The Truth about Hell 66

Chapter 8. Eternal Burning Hell – Fact or Fiction? 73

This is a picture of the statue in Nebuchadnezzar's dream, which represents Babylon, Medo-Persia, Greece, and Rome. Next to it is a picture of the beasts in Daniel's dream—the lion, the bear, the leopard, and the diverse fourth beast. Each set of symbols represents the same history.

Taken from *God Cares,* vol. 1, p. 106

Chapter 1

The Truth about the Little Horn Power

During the second year that Nebuchadnezzar II was king of Babylon, he had a dream that none of his counselors, advisors, magicians, or wise men could explain to him. However, Daniel, a young man who trusted God that had been brought from Judah to Babylon as a captive was able to tell the king what his dream was about.

Interestingly enough, years later, Daniel himself had a dream that covered the same history as Nebuchadnezzar's dream. It is amazing that God sent Daniel more information about what was going to happen in our world.

The purpose of Daniel's dream was to share the identity of the **little horn power**, which is also the Antichrist. This chapter is about the *truth* of the **little horn power,** also known as the **"*Antichrist,*"** which Daniel asked to understand.

Daniel was interested **only** in the *truth* of the visions, especially about the **little horn power,** which he refers to as the "***diverse***" beast. That is why, in verse 16, he asks for the *truth.* Then, in verse 19, he says that, by knowing the *truth* about the beasts, he will then know the *truth* about the **fourth beast** out of which the **little horn power** emerged.

Here is the chapter as a whole, with key elements emphasized in dark print.

Daniel 7:1-28

> In the first year of Belshazzar king of Babylon Daniel had a dream and **visions** of his head upon his bed: then he wrote the dream, and told the sum of the matters. ² Daniel spake and said, I saw in my vision by night, and, behold, the **four winds** of the heaven strove upon the great sea. ³ And **four great beasts** came up from **the sea,** diverse one from another. ⁴ The first was like a **lion,** and had **eagle's wings:** I beheld till the wings thereof were plucked, and it was lifted up from the earth, and made stand upon the feet as a man, and a man's heart was given to it. ⁵ And behold another beast, a second, like to a **bear,** and it **raised up itself on one side,**

and it had **three ribs** in the mouth of it between the teeth of it: and they said thus unto it, Arise, devour much flesh. ⁶ After this I beheld, and lo another, like a **leopard,** which had upon the back of it **four wings** of a fowl; the beast had also **four heads;** and dominion was given to it. ⁷ After this I saw in the night visions, and behold a **fourth beast, dreadful** and **terrible,** and **strong exceedingly;** and it had great **iron** teeth: it devoured and brake in pieces, and stamped the residue with the feet of it: and it was **diverse** from all the beasts that were before it; and it had **ten horns.** ⁸ I considered the horns, and, behold, there came up among them another **little horn,** before whom there were **three of the first horns plucked** up by the roots: and, behold, in this horn were eyes like the eyes of man, and a **mouth speaking** great things.

The Ancient of Days Reigns

⁹ I beheld till the thrones were cast down, and the Ancient of days did sit, whose garment was white as snow, and the hair of his head like the pure wool: his throne was like the fiery flame, and his wheels as burning fire. ¹⁰ A fiery stream issued and came forth from before him: thousand thousands ministered unto him, and ten thousand times ten thousand stood before him: the judgment was set, and the books were opened. ¹¹ I beheld then because of the voice of the **great words which the horn spake:** I beheld even till the beast was slain, and his body destroyed, and **given to the burning flame.** ¹² As concerning the rest of the beasts, they had their dominion taken away: yet their lives were prolonged for a season and time.

The Son of Man Is Given Dominion

¹³ I saw in the night visions, and, behold, one like the Son of man came with the clouds of heaven, and came to the Ancient of days, and they brought him near before him. ¹⁴ And there was given him dominion, and glory, and a kingdom, that all people, nations, and languages, should serve him: his dominion is an everlasting dominion, which shall not pass away, and his kingdom that which shall not be destroyed.

Daniel's Vision Interpreted

¹⁵ I Daniel was grieved in my spirit in the midst of my body, and the visions of my head **troubled me.** ¹⁶ I came near unto one of them that stood by, and asked him the truth **of all this.** So, he told me, and made me know the interpretation of the things. ¹⁷ These **great beasts,** which are four, are **four kings,** which shall arise out of the earth. ¹⁸ But the saints of the most High shall take the kingdom, and possess the kingdom

for ever, even for ever and ever. ¹⁹ Then I would know the *truth* *of the fourth beast,* which was *diverse* from all the others, exceeding dreadful, whose teeth were of iron, and his nails of brass; which devoured, brake in pieces, and stamped the residue with his feet; ²⁰ And of the **ten horns** that were in his head, and of **the other** which came up, and **before whom three fell;** even of that horn that had eyes, and a mouth that spake very great things, whose look was more stout than his fellows. ²¹ I beheld, and the *same horn* **made war with the saints,** and prevailed against them; ²² **Until the Ancient of days came,** and judgment was given to the saints of the most High; and the time came that the saints possessed the kingdom. ²³ Thus he said, The **fourth beast** shall be the **fourth kingdom** upon earth, which shall be **diverse from all kingdoms,** and shall devour the whole earth, and shall tread it down, and break it in pieces. ²⁴ And the ten horns out of this kingdom are **ten kings** that shall arise: and *another* shall rise **after them;** and he shall be **diverse from the first,** and he shall **subdue three kings.** ²⁵ And he shall **speak great words** *against* **the most High,** and shall wear out the saints of the most High, and **think to change times and laws:** and they shall be given into his hand until a **time and times and the dividing of time.** ²⁶ But the judgment shall sit, and they shall take away his dominion, to consume and to destroy it unto the end. ²⁷ And the kingdom and dominion, and the greatness of the kingdom under the whole heaven, shall be given to the people of the saints of the most High, whose kingdom is an everlasting kingdom, and all dominions shall serve and obey him. ²⁸ Hitherto is the end of the matter. As for me Daniel, my cogitations much troubled me, and my countenance changed in me: but I kept the matter in my heart.

> *If someone speaks against Christ, he is "antichrist."*

Verse 22 reveals that this **little horn power** will be working **against Jesus** until the **end of time** when Jesus returns. When the statement is made that the "saints will possess the kingdom," it refers to Jesus' second coming when we go to heaven with Him.

Verse 25 states that this **little horn power** will speak "great words against the most High." If someone speaks against Christ, he is *"antichrist."*

As **chapter 7** begins, Daniel sees **four beasts** coming up out of the **sea.**

In **prophecy,** a beast represents a **king and his kingdom** such as *Alexander the Great* from **Greece** who was represented by the third beast in Daniel's vision.

> These great beasts, which are four, are **four kings,** which shall arise out of the earth. (Dan. 7:17)

In **prophecy,** the **sea** represents populated areas of the world. The King James Version states it this way:

> And he saith unto me, The waters which thou sawest, where the whore sitteth, are **peoples,** and **multitudes,** and **nations,** and **tongues.** (Rev. 17:15)

The Contemporary English Version uses the words "**crowds of people.**"

> The oceans that you saw the prostitute sitting on are **crowds of people** from all races and languages. (Rev. 17:15, CEV)

So, the **four beasts** of Daniel 7 represent four kingdoms coming up out of **populated areas** of the world, which, back in 550 BC, was in the Middle East.

Nebuchadnezzar II, who was represented by the **first beast,** ruled the world, from **605 to 562 BC** from the city of Babylon, which is located along the Euphrates River in present-day Iraq, about 50 miles south of Baghdad. This was the most populated part of the world in those days.

Verse 4 refers to the first **beast, or kingdom,** as a **lion.** When Daniel interpreted **Nebuchadnezzar's** dream in Daniel 2, the first kingdom, a **head of gold,** represented **Babylon.** In Daniel's dream, recorded in chapter 7, the first kingdom is a **lion,** which also represented **Babylon.**

The "**eagle's wings**" of the lion represent the beast's speed in conquest, as we see in **Deuteronomy 28:49,** which says, "The LORD shall bring a nation against thee from far, from the end of the earth, as **swift** as the eagle flieth; a nation whose tongue thou shalt not understand."

Verse 2 speaks of "**four winds.**" These **winds** represent **strife and destruction.** The King James Version of **Jeremiah 25:32, 33** says, "Thus saith the LORD of hosts, Behold, evil shall go forth from nation to nation, and a **great whirlwind** shall be raised up from the coasts of the earth. [33] And the slain of the LORD shall be at that day from one end of the earth even unto the other end of the earth: they shall not be lamented, neither gathered, nor buried; they shall be dung upon the ground."

The second beast in Daniel's dream is a **bear** with **three ribs** in its mouth. It represents the second kingdom of **Medo-Persia.**

In Daniel chapter 8, we see that beasts in chapter 8 parallel the beasts in chapter 7. **Daniel 8:20** specifically names **Medo-Persia** as the kingdom that precedes the male goat that is Greece in verse 21.

Medo-Persia is the **second kingdom,** the same power as the bear of Daniel 7. This empire was made up of *two people groups.* The first of these to arise were the Medes, which are represented, in **Daniel 7:5,** by the bear raised up on one side. However, if you study ancient history, the Persians eventually became stronger than the Medes. The Medes are represented in **Daniel 8:3** by the ram's **second horn** that grew **"higher."**

The three ribs in the bear's mouth represent the three principal powers conquered by Medo-Persia: **Lydia, Babylon, and Egypt.**

The **Leopard Beast** of Daniel 7 represents the world kingdom of **Greece.**

Greece, the third kingdom (Dan. 8:21), is represented by a leopard with *four wings* and *four heads* (Dan. 7:6).

The *four wings* (instead of two, as the lion had) represent the incredible speed with which Alexander conquered the ancient world (Jer. 4:11–13).

The UShistory.org web site states, regarding Alexander the Great: "A great conqueror, in 13 short years, he amassed the *largest empire* in the entire ancient world—an empire that covered 3,000 miles. And he did this without the benefit of modern technology and weaponry. In his day, troop movements were primarily on foot, and communications were face to face. Not bad for a kid who became the King of Macedon at the age of 20" ("Alexander the Great, UShistory.org, https://1ref.us/22i, accessed Sept. 22, 2022).

The four heads of the third beast represent the *four kingdoms* into which the empire of Alexander the Great was divided when he died. The four generals who headed these areas were **Cassander, Lysimachus, Ptolemy,** and **Seleucus.**

The Roman Empire, the *fourth kingdom,* is represented by a powerful monster with iron teeth and ten horns (Dan. 7:7).

The *ten horns* represent the ten kings, or kingdoms, into which **pagan Rome** was eventually split (Dan. 7:24). These ten kingdoms are the same as the *feet and toes* of the image described in Daniel 2:41–44.

In 476 A.D., Romulus, the last of the Roman emperors in the west, was overthrown by the Germanic leader Odoacer, who became the first Barbarian to rule in Rome. The order that the Roman Empire had brought to western Europe for 1000 years was no more. It was these **barbarian tribes** that conquered the Roman Empire, dividing its territories into separate "countries" for their people. Seven of those ten tribes developed into the countries of modern **Western Europe.** However, three of the **"new"** countries were **"uprooted"** and destroyed.

The ten tribes that Rome was split into were:

1. The Visigoths – **Spain**
2. The Anglo-Saxons – **England**
3. The Franks – **France**
4. The Alemanni – **Germany**
5. The Burgundians – **Switzerland**
6. The Lombards – **Italy**
7. The Suevi – **Portugal**
8. *The Heruli* – Destroyed, or **uprooted**
9. *The Ostrogoths* – Destroyed, or **uprooted**
10. *The Vandals* – Destroyed, or **uprooted**

As noted, tribes eight through ten were destroyed, or uprooted, by the little horn power. These tribes were the **Heruli,** the **Ostrogoths,** and the **Vandals.** Search on the names of any of these three tribes on the internet, and you will find the history of their destruction. History confirms all of the Bible's prophecies.

Now, for the **little horn power** that became the *Antichrist*.

In verse 8, Daniel says that, among the **ten horns,** which are kingdoms, another **little horn** arose which **destroyed three** of the first ten horns, that is, the Heruli, Ostrogoths, and Vandals.

> I considered the horns, and, behold, there came up among them another **little horn,** before whom there were **three of the first horns plucked up by the roots:** and, behold, in this horn were eyes like the eyes of man, and a mouth speaking great things. (Dan. 7:8)

We must consider the biblical characteristics carefully because they identify the **"little horn"** as the **Antichrist** of prophecy and history. There must be no mistake in making the identification.

God's Word gives us *nine characteristics* of the *little horn power* (the Antichrist) in Daniel 7.

1. The little horn would come **"up among them"**—that is, from among the ten horns that were the kingdoms of Western Europe (Dan. 7:8). This means that it would be a *little kingdom* somewhere in *Western Europe* and that it would arise *after* Rome was taken over by the ten tribes.

2. It would have *a man at its head* who could speak for it (Dan. 7:8).

3. It would *pluck out, or uproot, three kingdoms* that preceded it (Dan. 7:8).

4. It would be *different* from the other ten kingdoms (Dan. 7:24).

5. It would *make war with* and *persecute the saints* (Dan. 7:21, 25).

6. It would *emerge from the pagan Roman Empire*—the fourth kingdom (Dan. 7:7, 8).

7. God's people ("the saints") would **"be given into his hand"** for **"a time and times and half a time"** (Dan. 7:25). Later, we will see how "a time, times, and half a time" means 1,260 years.

8. It would **"speak great words against,"** or blaspheme, **God** (Dan. 7:25). In Revelation 13:5, the Bible says the same power speaks "great things and blasphemies."

9. It would **"think to change times and laws"** (Dan. 7:25).

All nine of these identification points come directly from the Bible. They are not some human opinion or speculation. **Historians** prove very quickly what power is being described because these points fit only **one power,** and we will see that that one power is *the papacy.* However, that we may be certain of this identification, let us carefully examine all nine points one by one. There must be no room left for doubt.

1. ***It came up among the ten kingdoms of Western Europe.***

   The geographical location of the **papal** power *is in Rome, Italy*—in the heart of **Western Europe.** So that is the ***first fact*** that points to the little horn as symbolizing the Roman Catholic Church.

2. ***It would have a man at its head who speaks for it.***

   The papacy meets this identifying mark because it does have one man at the head—*the pope*—who speaks for it. So, this is the ***second fact*** that it could be the Roman Catholic Church.

3. ***Three kingdoms were plucked up to make way for the rise of the papacy.***

   The emperors of Western Europe were largely Catholic and supported the papacy. **Three Arian kingdoms, however,** *did not support the papacy*. These were the **Vandals,** the **Heruli,** and the **Ostrogoths.** So, the **Catholic emperors** decided they must be subdued or destroyed.

   Here is how theologian and historian **Dr. Mervyn Maxwell** describes the results in his book, *God Cares:*

   > **The Catholic emperor Zeno** (474–491) arranged a treaty with the Ostrogoths in 487 which resulted in the eradication of the kingdom of the Arian *Heruls* in 493. And the Catholic emperor Justinian (527–565) exterminated the Arian *Vandals* in 534 and significantly broke the power of the Arian *Ostrogoths* in 538. Thus were **Daniel's three horns,** the **Heruls,** the **Vandals,** and the **Ostrogoths**— "plucked up by the roots." (*God Cares*, vol. 1, p. 129)

   > ***It is not difficult to recognize that the papacy fits this point.*** This ***fact alone*** proves that the little horn power is the Roman Catholic Church. History proves that it was the Catholic Church that defeated these three kingdoms.

4. ***It would be*** **different** ***from the other kingdoms.***

   The papacy clearly fits this description as well, as it came on the scene as a **religious power** and was therefore different from the **secular nature** of the other ten kingdoms.

Although being "religious," it ruled over the kings of Europe. The Catholic Church felt that it had the right to hold dominion over the entire world, including all kings. Here is a quotation from the Catholic Church itself stating this fact:

> **"We define that the Holy Apostolic See and the Roman Pontiff hold the primacy over the whole world"** (A Decree of the Council of Trent, quoted in Philippe Labbé and Gabriel Cossart, *Sacrosancta Concilia Ad Regiam Editionem Exacta* [The Most Holy Councils Exacted for the Royal Edition], vol. 13, col. 1167, English translation, available at https://1ref.us/22k, accessed Sept. 22, 2022; Latin, available at https://1ref.us/22l, accessed Sept. 22, 2022).

5. **It would make war with** and **persecute the saints.**

The fact that the Catholic Church did persecute Christians is a well-known fact, and the papacy admits doing so. Historians believe the church destroyed at least **50 million lives** over matters of **religious conviction.**

6. It would **emerge from the fourth kingdom of iron, the pagan Roman Empire.**

Here are two statements from authorities on this point:

> The mighty Catholic Church was little more than the Roman Empire baptised. Rome was transformed as well as converted. The very capital of the old Roman Empire became the capital of the Christian empire. The office of **Pontifex Maximus** was continued in that of **pope.** (Alexander Clarence Flick, *The Rise of the Mediaeval Church,* 1909, pp. 148, 149)

> Whatever Roman elements the barbarians and Arians left standing in the provinces—and they were few—were ecclesiastical and at the same time put under the protection of the Bishop of Rome, who was the chief person there after the emperor's disappearance. ... The Roman church ... pushed itself into the place of the Roman World-Empire, of which it is the actual continuation; the empire has not perished, but has only undergone a transformation. (Adolf Harnack, *What Is Christianity?* 1901, pp. 269, 270, available at https://1ref.us/22m, accessed Sept. 22, 2022)

7. *God's people (the saints) would* **"be given into his hand"** *for* **"a time and times and half** *a time."*

Several things need clarification here:

a. ***A time is a year; times is two years; half a time is half of a year.*** In Daniel 12:7, it says, "And I heard the man clothed in linen, which was upon the waters of the river, when he held up his right hand and his left hand unto heaven, and sware by him that liveth for ever that it shall be for a time, times, and an half; and when he shall have accomplished to scatter the power of the holy people, all these things shall be finished."

   This same time frame is also spoken of in **Revelation 12:14,** where the "woman" (a symbol of the church) flees from the dragon (a symbol of Satan) for the same time. Here are the same two verses written in a modern translation of the Bible.

   > The angel raised both hands toward the sky and made a solemn promise in the name of the Eternal God. I heard him say, "It will be ***three and a half years.*** When the persecution of God's people ends, all these things will have happened." (Dan. 12:7, GNT)

   > She was given the two wings of a large eagle in order to fly to her place in the desert, where she will be taken care of for ***three and a half years,*** safe from the dragon's attack. (Rev. 12:14, GNT)

b. This same time period is mentioned seven times in the books of Daniel and Revelation (Dan. 7:25; 12:7; Rev. 11:2, 3; 12:6, 14; 13:5)—three of these times as a "time, times, and half a time," two times as 42 months, and two times as 1,260 days. Based on the 30-day calendar used by the Jews, these time periods are all the same amount of time:

   3½ years = 42 months = ***1,260 days.***

c. Two other passages show that one ***prophetic day*** equals ***one literal year*** (Ezek. 4:6; Num. 14:34).

d. Thus, the little horn (or Antichrist) was to ***have power*** over the saints for 1,260 prophetic days, or ***1,260 literal years.***

e. The *rule of the papacy* began in ***538 AD,*** when the last of the three opposing Arian kingdoms were uprooted. Its rule continued until ***1798 AD*** when Napoleon's general, Berthier, took the pope captive with the hope of destroying both Pope Pius VI and the political power of the papacy. ***This period of time is an exact fulfillment of the 1,260-year prophecy.*** The blow was a deadly wound for the papacy, but that wound begin to heal and continues healing today.

f. This same period of persecution is mentioned in Matthew 24:21 as the worst period of **persecution God's people** ever experience. Verse 22 tells us it was so devastating that not one soul would have survived if God had not shortened it. But God did shorten it, and the persecution ended long before the pope was taken captive in 1798. It is plain to see that this point, likewise, *fits the papacy.*

8. *The little horn power is said to speak "pompous words" of blasphemy "against" God.* Blasphemy has two definitions in Scripture:

    a. Claiming to *forgive sins,* which God only can do (Luke 5:21).

    b. Claiming to *be God* (John 10:33).

Do these two points fit the papacy? Absolutely, Yes! Let's first look at the evidence for the Catholic Church claiming to forgive sins, taken directly from its own literature:

> *Seek where you will, through heaven and earth, and you will find but one created being who can* forgive the sinner *... that extraordinary being is the priest, the [Roman]* Catholic priest*.* (Michael Muller, *The Catholic Priest,* pp. 78, 79, quoted in Mary Ellen Walsh, *The Wine of Roman Babylon,* 1945, p. 14, available at https://1ref.us/22n, accessed Sept. 22, 2022)

Not only do they claim to be able to forgive sins, but they say that God has to abide by their decisions. In other words, they claim that they are above God. Here is their own statement:

> *God himself is obliged to abide by the judgment of his priests, and either not to pardon or to pardon, according as they refuse or give absolution, provided the penitent is capable of it. ... The sentence of the priest precedes, and God subscribes to it.* (Alfonso Maria de Liguori, *Dignity and Duties of the Priest,* 1888, p. 27, available at https://1ref.us/22o, accessed Sept. 22, 2022)

Now let's see the evidence that the pope is claiming he is God:

> *We hold upon this earth the place of God Almighty.* (Pope Leo XIII, Encyclical Letter, "The Reunion of Christendom," dated June 20, 1894)

> *The Pope is not only the representative of Jesus Christ, but he is Jesus Christ Himself, hidden under veil of flesh.* (Cardinal Joseph Melchiorre Sarto, Archbishop of Venice, who became Pope Pius X, *Le Catholique National,* July 13, 1895, in *The Friend,* Dec. 7, 1895, p. 154, available at https://1ref.us/22p, accessed Sept. 22, 2022)

The last characteristic of the **little horn power** that the angel gave to Daniel is about its intending to **change times and laws.** God's ten commandments are His laws, and the only one with time is the fourth commandment.

9. **It would "think to *change times and laws.*"**

Again, let's let the Catholic Church itself prove that they did do this.

> It was the **Catholic Church** which, by the authority of Jesus Christ, has **transferred this rest** [from the Bible Sabbath] to the Sunday in remembrance of the resurrection of our Lord. Thus the observance of Sunday by the Protestants is an homage they pay, in spite of themselves, to the **authority** of the [Catholic] Church. (Monsignor Louis Gaston de Ségur, *Plain Talk about the Protestantism of To-day,* 1808, p. 225, at https://1ref.us/22q, accessed Sept. 22, 2022)

> We observe Sunday instead of Saturday because the **Catholic Church** transferred the solemnity from Saturday to Sunday. (Peter Geiermann, CSSR, *The Convert's Catechism of Catholic Doctrine,* 1957 edition, p. 50)

In Chapter 3, there are dozens more Catholic statements in which Catholic authorities claim to have changed the Sabbath to Sunday.

Not only did they think they **changed the Sabbath** from the seventh day to the first day, but they also changed the **Ten Commandments** in their catechisms by deleting the second commandment that declares: "Thou shalt not make unto thee any graven image" (Exod. 20:4).

They deleted it all together and then **split the tenth commandment** in two between "Thou shalt not covet thy neighbor's wife" and "Thou shalt not covet thy neighbor's goods" so that they could still have ten commandments. One of these changes times; the two together change laws.

There is no doubt that the **little horn power,** the Antichrist, of Daniel 7 is the *papacy.* No other organization fits **all nine points God gave Daniel.** And, incidentally, this is not a new teaching. *Every* **Protestant Reformer,** without exception, spoke of the papacy as Antichrist. (We will see examples later.)

9. **Was Daniel told to seal up his book "until the time of the end" (Dan. 12:4)?**

Yes, in **Daniel 12:4,** the prophet was told to seal the book till the **"time of the end."** In verse 6, an angelic voice asked, "How long shall the fulfillment of these wonders be?" The response in verse 7 is: "It shall be for **a time, times, and half a time."** The angel assured Daniel that the section of the book dealing with end-time prophecies would be opened after the end of the 1,260-year period of papal control, which was, as we learned earlier, **1798.** So, the time of the end began in the year 1798.

As we have seen, the book of Daniel contains ***crucial messages*** from heaven ***for us today.*** We must understand it, and all religious teachings must be compared with Scripture to determine their accuracy.

10. ***Many Christians today have been misinformed regarding the*** Antichrist. To believe an untruth about the Antichrist causes a person to be deceived. We are told that we must prove everything we hear from the Bible itself so we can find out if what we are told is true.

11. The statement that confirms that principle is in Acts: "These were more fair-minded than those in Thessalonica, in that they received the word with all readiness, and ***searched the Scriptures daily*** to find out whether ***these things were so***" (Acts 17:11, NKJV).

    The ***real question*** is: are we interested in the "*truth*?" Are we willing to follow where Jesus leads, following the "***truth,***" even though it might be painful and go against what we have been told our entire lives?

    > *Daniel contains crucial messages from heaven for us today. We must understand it.*

    John, who wrote the book of ***Revelation,*** even states the importance of truth. It was because of his decision to tell the truth about Jesus that he was sent to Patmos as a criminal.

    > I am John, your brother, and as a follower of Jesus I am your partner in *patiently enduring* **the** *suffering* that comes to those **who belong to his Kingdom.** I was put on the island of Patmos **because** I had proclaimed God's word and the *truth* that Jesus revealed. (Rev. 1:9, GNT)

The prophecy of Daniel is also the truth. It undoubtedly proves that the Roman Catholic Church is the **little horn power,** the **Antichrist,** who has deceived the entire world. Their *deception* includes changing the **Sabbath** to **Sunday,** which **99.92%** of the Christian world today follows.

My entire life, I have wondered how the vast majority of people around the world could be deceived about the **"*truth*"** as it is stated in God's Holy Word.

The **Catholic Church,** the Papacy, believes that they control the entire world. They believe that they have more authority than Jesus Himself in that their tradition is equal to what the Bible teaches. They changed the **Ten Commandments;** they changed the ***day of worship.*** They instituted purgatory.

They took over the act of forgiveness through the Pope and his priests, claiming that Jesus has to abide by their decisions. The **pope claims** to be Jesus Himself.

They claim that their communion service through Transubstantiation changes the substances of the bread and wine into the actual substance of the body and blood of Christ.

Catholics believe all of this due to their decision at the Council of Trent where they voted that "***Scripture and** tradition* are to be received and venerated equally."

My biggest question is this: As Protestants, who understand that none of these Catholic *"traditions"* are Biblical, why then do we follow the Catholic Church's **tradition** of worshiping on **Sunday** instead of the **Biblical Sabbath that Jesus created when He created our world?**

Especially is this true when the **Catholic Church itself** claims that they are the ones who changed the day of worship from Sabbath to Sunday and not Jesus. They also claim that those who worship on Sunday are ***following the Catholic Church*** and not *Jesus*.

My only answer is found in the words of Jesus, where He teaches that *only a few* people will find the true path (***Matthew 7:13, 14***). ***Sunday*** is followed by the entire world, yet the ***seventh-day Sabbath,*** which God made on the seventh day of creation, is followed by *only a few*.

You may wonder why we should study about the ***Antichrist.*** It is because Bible prophecies teach that the ***Antichrist*** power will play a crucial role in the ***final events*** of earth's history.

We cannot understand ***last-day events*** until we understand this *evil* power known as the ***Antichrist.*** The Antichrist is the **little horn power** of Daniel 7, which is the **Roman Catholic Church.**

So you can understand the Antichrist is why I shared the study of the entire chapter of Daniel 7. By studying Daniel 7, we learn that the **little horn power** is the last beast covered by Daniel's vision. Daniel 7 reveals that *the Antichrist is the papacy,* which **all Protestants** in the 1500s including **Martin Luther** (1483–1546) believed.

Here is Martin Luther's statement r egarding the Pope being Antichrist:

> **The Pope** is the very ***Antichrist,*** who has exalted himself above, and opposed himself against Christ because he will not permit Christians to be saved without his power, which, nevertheless, is nothing, and is neither ordained nor commanded by God. (The Smalcald Articles, II, IV)

French Protestant reformer John Calvin (1509–1564) also identified the Antichrist:

It is certain that the **Roman Pontiff** has impudently transferred to himself the most peculiar properties of God and Christ, there cannot be a doubt that he is the leader and standard-bearer of an impious and abominable kingdom ... Although the Pope, **who is Antichrist,** be set in God's sanctuary ... he is not worthy to be taken and accounted for a minister. (*Institutes of the Christian Religion,* vol. 4)

Scottish theologian John Knox (1514-1572) also identified the "man of sin":

Yea, to speak it in plain words; lest that we submit ourselves to Satan, thinking that we submit ourselves to Jesus Christ; for, as for your **Roman kirk, as it is now corrupted,** and the authority thereof, whereon stands the hope of your victory, I no more doubt but that it is the synagogue of Satan, and the head thereof, called the pope, to be that **man of sin,** of whom the apostle speaks. (John Knox, *The History of the Reformation of Religion in Scotland,* book 1, 1831, p. 65, available at https://1ref.us/22r, accessed Sept. 22, 2022)

Leader of the English Reformation and Archbishop of Canterbury Thomas Cranmer (1489-1556) likewise identified the Antichrist:

Whereof it followeth Rome to be the seat of **antichrist,** and **the pope** to be very antichrist himself. I could prove the same by many other scriptures, other writers, and strong reasons. (*Miscellaneous Writings and Letters of Thomas Cranmer,* vol. 1, 1844, p. 63, available at https://1ref.us/22s, accessed Sept. 22, 2022)

Additional Statements Written after the 1500s

English theologian and founder of the Methodists John Wesley (1703-1791) wrote:

[The Pope] is, in an emphatical sense, the man of sin, as he increases all manner of sin above measure. And he is too properly styled, The son of perdition, as he has caused the death of numberless multitudes, both of his opposers and followers, destroyed innumerable souls, and will himself perish everlastingly. He it is that opposeth himself to the emperor, once his rightful sovereign; and that exalteth himself above all that is called God, or that is worshipped—Commanding angels, and putting kings under his feet, both of whom are called gods in Scripture: claiming the highest power, the highest honour; suffering himself not once only to be styled God or vice-god. Indeed, no less is implied in his ordinary title, Most holy lord or Most holy father. So that he sitteth—Enthroned, in the temple of God—Mentioned Rev. xi, 1, **declaring himself that he is God**—Claiming the prerogatives which belong to God alone. (John Wesley, *Explanatory Notes upon the New Testament*, 1813, pp. 534, 535, available at https://1ref.us/22t, accessed Sept. 22, 2022)

Scottish historian of religion J. A. Wylie (1808-1890) wrote:

In the life of Christ we behold the converse of what the Antichrist must be; and in the prophecy of the Antichrist we are shown the converse of what Christ must be, and was. And when we place the Papacy between the two, and compare it with each, we find, on the one hand, that it is the perfect converse of Christ as seen in His life; and, on the other, that it is the **perfect image of the Antichrist,** as shown in the prophecy of him. We conclude, therefore, that if Jesus of Nazareth be the Christ, the **Roman Papacy is the Antichrist.** (J. A. Wylie, *The Papacy Is the Antichrist: A Demonstration,* 1888, p. iv, available at https://1ref.us/22u, accessed Sept. 22, 2022)

Famed Baptist preacher Charles Spurgeon (1834-1892) wrote:

It is the duty of every Christian to **pray against Antichrist,** and as to what Antichrist is no sane man ought to raise a question. If it be not the Popery in the Church of Rome and in the Church of England, there is nothing in the world that can be called by that name. If there were to be issued a hue and cry for Antichrist, we should certainly take up those two churches on suspicion, and they certainly would not be let loose again, for they so exactly answer the description. **Popery anywhere, whether it be Anglican or Romish, is contrary to Christ's gospel,** and **is the Antichrist,** and we ought to pray against it. It should be the daily prayer of every believer that Antichrist might be hurled like a millstone into the flood and sink to rise no more. If we can pray against error for Christ because it wounds Christ, because it robs Christ of his glory, because it puts sacramental efficacy in the place of His atonement, and lifts a piece of bread into the place of the Savior, and a few drops of water into the place of the Holy Spirit, and puts a mere fallible man like ourselves up as the vicar of Christ on earth. (C. H. Spurgeon, "Pray for Jesus," *Spurgeon's Sermons,* vol. XII, 1866, pp. 994, 995, available at https://1ref.us/22v, accessed Sept. 22, 2022)

So, if the pope is ***truly the Antichrist,*** then he is **Satan's** right-hand man, and we cannot follow him and his beliefs, the most significant of which is ***worshiping on Sunday.***

Chapter 2

The Council of Trent

The Protestant Reformation was a religious reform movement that swept through Europe in the 1500s. It resulted in the creation of a branch of Christianity called Protestantism, a name used collectively to refer to the many religious groups that separated from the Roman Catholic Church due to differences in doctrine. They wanted to follow the ***Bible and the Bible only!***

The ***Protestant Reformation*** began in Wittenberg, Germany, on October 31, 1517, when *Martin Luther,* a teacher and a monk, published a document he called Disputation on the Power of Indulgences, which is commonly called the "95 Theses." The document was a series of ninety-five ideas about Christianity that he invited people to debate with him. These ideas were controversial because they directly contradicted the Catholic Church's teachings.

Luther's statements challenged the Catholic Church's role as intermediary between the people and God, specifically as it had to do with the system of indulgences, which, in part, allowed people to purchase a certificate of pardon for the punishment of their sins.

Luther argued against the practice of buying or earning forgiveness, believing instead that salvation is a gift that God gives to those who have faith. There was a strong party, even among the Catholics in the council, who were in favor of ***abandoning tradition*** and adopting ***the Scriptures only*** as the standard of authority.

Because the Protestants wanted to leave the ***tradition*** of the Roman Catholic Church, the *Council of Trent* was created to fight against the Protestants who wanted to follow the Bible, and the Bible only, and destroy them.

Because of these two groups of Catholics, the *Council of Trent* was a debate between "Scripture alone" and "Scripture plus *tradition*."

But to move towards the Bible alone would also manifestly go a long way towards justifying the claims of the Protestants. The crisis pushed the ultra-Catholic part of the council to have to convince the others that "**Scripture and tradition**" were the only sure ground to stand upon. If this could be done, the council could be carried to issue a decree **condemning the Reformation.** Otherwise, they could not. The question was debated over the span of *eighteen years* until the council was brought almost to a standstill.

Finally, after a long and intensive mental strain, the **Archbishop of Reggio** came into the council with substantially the following argument to the party who held for *Scripture alone*. He said to the council:

> The Protestants **claim** to stand upon the **written word only.** They profess to hold the **Scripture alone** as the standard of faith. They justify their revolt by the plea that the Church has apostatized from the written word and follows tradition. Now the Protestants' claim that they stand upon the written word only, *is not true.* Their profession of holding the Scripture alone as the standard of faith, **is false. PROOF:** The written word explicitly enjoins the observance of the **seventh day** as the **Sabbath.** They do not observe the seventh day but reject it. If they do truly hold the Scripture alone as their standard, they would be observing the seventh

> *If they do truly hold the Scripture alone as their standard, they would be observing the seventh day as is enjoined in the Scripture throughout.*

day as is enjoined in the Scripture throughout. **Yet they not only reject the observance of the Sabbath enjoined in the written word, but they have adopted and do practice the observance of Sunday, for which they have only the tradition of the Church.** ("The Council of Trent," Sabbath Truth, https://1ref.us/22h, accessed Sept. 22, 2022)

It was because of the **Archbishop of Reggio's** comment that Protestants who claimed to follow the Scripture alone but still observed Sunday were following Catholic tradition that the position of *Scripture alone* lost and the position of *Scripture plus tradition* won.

Chapter 3

Sabbath or Sunday?

In this chapter we will review a number of statements made by the Roman Catholic Church on this crucial subject. We will begin with a statement about *the first Sunday law.*

Early in 321 A.D., the Roman Emperor Constantine issued a decree known as **"The Edict of Constantine,"** which made *Sunday* a public festival throughout the Roman Empire. The decree reads:

> On the venerable Day of the Sun let the magistrates and people residing in cities rest, and let all workshops be closed. In the country, however, persons engaged in agriculture may freely and lawfully continue their pursuits; because it often happens that another day is not so suitable for grain-sowing or for vine-planting; lest by neglecting the proper moment for such operations, the bounty of heaven should be lost. (Given the 7th day of March, Crispus and Constantine being consuls each of them for the second time.) (Philip Schaff, *History of the Christian Church,* 1889, vol. 3, chap. 5, sec. 75, p. 380, available at https://1ref.us/22w, accessed Sept. 22, 2022).

Like Aurelian and Diocletian before him, Constantine was a worshiper of the sun. He was also the first emperor to profess belief in Christianity. **The day of the sun (Sun-day) was reverenced or considered holy by his pagan subjects and was also honored by some Christians in Rome and Alexandria.**

The emperor Constantine, who was trying to unite his pagan and Christian subjects was urged to do this by the bishops of the Roman Church, believing that this way they could **advance the power** and prestige of the **Roman Catholic Church.**

It seems that Constantine's personal religion was a mixture of Mithraic *sun worship* and Christianity. According to his Christian biographer, Eusebius,

Constantine taught all his armies to zealously honor Sunday as the Lord's Day, and he referred to it as **"the day of light and of the sun."** This was distinctly **pagan terminology.**

For Christians today, it may seem ironic that the first Sunday law, the famous Edict of Constantine, uses the language of *sun worshipers* rather than Christian expressions. In the edict, the first day of the week is exalted as "the venerable day of the sun" with no mention of Christ or of celebrating His resurrection. ***Thus, the first Sunday law had no Christian flavor whatsoever.***

> *It seems that Constantine's personal religion was a mixture of Mithraic sun worship and Christianity.*

For many years, I have collected **Catholic quotations** that establish that they are the ones who claim to have changed the Sabbath to Sunday and *not God!* However, if someone is a **Christian,** then they follow **Jesus Christ** and His teachings in the Bible. When people began following Jesus Christ after His resurrection and were then called Christians, they started keeping the *seventh-day Sabbath* that Jesus created back when He created the world.

Amazingly, in the early Middle Ages, the Catholic Church claimed they had discovered letters from heaven declaring that the day of rest had been changed by God so that they could frighten Christians into observing Sunday rather than the Sabbath.

Also, in 1054, Pope Leo IX excommunicated the entire Eastern Orthodox Church, partly because the Orthodox Church celebrated the Sabbath. *Of all the churches in the world, the church of Rome became the one that opposed the seventh-day Sabbath the most.*

The following quotations are from assorted Catholic journals relating to Sunday worship and the Catholic Church's belief that they had the right to change it from Sabbath to Sunday! The first nine quotations explain why the Catholic Church believed their power was such that they could change God's laws.

Catholic Quotations

> We define that the Holy Apostolic See, and the Roman Pontiff, hold the *primacy over the whole world.* (A Decree of the Council of Trent, quoted in Labbé and Cossart, *Sacrosancta Concilia* [The Most Holy Councils], vol. 13, col. 1167)

The church may by divine right confiscate the property of heretics, imprison their person, and condemn them to the flames. In our age, the right to inflict the severest penalties, even death, belongs to the church. There is no graver offense than heresy, therefore it must be rooted out. (*Public Ecclesiastical Law,* vol. 2, p. 142)

We hold upon this earth **the place of God Almighty.** (Pope Leo XIII, "To the Rulers and Nations of the World," an encyclical letter dated June 20, 1894, in *The American Catholic Quarterly Review,* October 1894, p. 778, available at https://1ref.us/22x, accessed Sept. 22, 2022)

The Pope is not only the representative of Jesus Christ, but *he is Jesus Christ Himself,* hidden under the veil of flesh. (Cardinal Joseph Melchiorre Sarto, *Le Catholique National,* July 13, 1895)

The Pope is of so great dignity and so exalted that he is not a mere man, but as it were God, and **the vicar of God.**

He is likewise the divine monarch and supreme emperor and king of kings … so that if it be possible that the **angels might err** the faith, they **could be judged** and **excommunicated** by the pope. (Lucius Ferraris, *Prompta Bibliotheca,* vol. VI, "Papa II")

Seek where you will, through Heaven and earth, and you will find but one **created being** who can **forgive the sinner** … That extraordinary being is the priest, the Roman Catholic priest. (*The Catholic Priest,* pp. 78, 79)

God Himself is obliged to abide by the judgment of his priests, and either not to pardon or to pardon, according as they refuse or give absolution, provided the penitent is capable of it. 'Such is,' says St. Maximus of Turin, 'this judiciary power ascribed to Peter that its decision carries with it the decision of God.' The sentence of the priest precedes, and *God subscribes to it.* (Alfonso Maria de Saint Liguori, *Dignity and Duties of the Priest,* 1888, p. 27, available at https://1ref.us/22y, accessed Sept. 22, 2022)

The pope can modify divine law, since his power is not of man, but of God, and he acts in the place of God upon earth, with the fullest power of binding and loosing his sheep. (Petrus de Ancharano, in Lucius Ferraris, *Prompta Bibliotheca,* vol. 6, 1772, p. 29, art. 2, "Papa")

These first statements show what *power* the Catholic Church believes it has. This is why they made the statements that follow about worshiping God on Sunday and not on the seventh-day Sabbath on the basis of their power!

The Catholic Church actually believes, if you are a true Protestant, which means a Christian who is not a Catholic but follows the Bible as the rule of faith and practice, that you should not be worshiping God on Sunday with them and that you are a heretic that needs to be punished.

> **Not the Creator** of the Universe, in Genesis 2:1–3, but the Catholic Church "can claim the honor of having granted man **a pause to his work every seven days.** (Corrado S. Mosna, *Storia della Domenica dalle origini fino agli inizi del V secolo,* 1969, pp. 366, 367)
>
> It was the Catholic Church which, by the authority of Jesus Christ, has transferred this rest [from the Bible Sabbath] to the Sunday … Thus the **observance of Sunday** by the Protestants is *an homage they pay, in spite of themselves,* to the authority of the [Catholic] Church. (Monsignor Louis Gaston de Ségur, *Plain Talk about the Protestantism of To-day,* p. 225)
>
> We observe Sunday instead of Saturday because *the Catholic Church in the council of Laodicea transferred the solemnity from Saturday to Sunday.* (Peter Geiermann, CSSR, *The Catechism of Catholic Doctrine,* 1957 edition, p. 50)
>
> The Church changed the observance of the Sabbath to Sunday by right of the divine, infallible authority given to her by her founder, Jesus Christ. *The Protestant claiming the Bible to be the only guide of faith has no warrant for observing Sunday.* In this matter the Seventh Day Adventist is the only consistent Protestant. ("The Question Box," *The Catholic Universe Bulletin,* Aug. 14, 1942, p. 4)
>
> The Bible says, "*Remember* that thou keep holy the Sabbath day." The Catholic Church says, "*No.* by my divine power *I abolish the Sabbath day* and *command you to keep holy the first day of the week.*" And lo! the entire civilized world bows down in reverent obedience to the command of the Holy Catholic Church. (Father Thomas Enright, President of Redemptorist College, in a lecture at Hartford, Kansas, Feb. 18, 1884)
>
> God simply gave His [the Catholic] Church the power to set aside whatever day or days, she would deem suitable as Holy Days. *The Church chose Sunday,* the first day of the week, and in the course of time added other days, as holy days. (Vincent J. Kelly, *Forbidden Sunday and Feast-day Occupations,* 1943, p. 2)

Sunday is a Catholic institution, and its claims to observance can be defended only on Catholic principles … **From beginning to end of scripture there is not a single passage that warrants the transfer of weekly public worship from the last day of the week to the first.** (*Catholic Press,* Sydney, Australia, August 1900)

The authority of the Church could therefore not be bound to the authority of Scriptures, because the Church had changed … the Sabbath into Sunday, **not by command of Christ, but buy its *own authority*.** (Pope John Paul II, *Canon and Tradition,* p. 263)

A person who *violates the sanctity of Sunday* is to be punished as a heretic. (*Detroit News,* July 7, 1998, p. A1)

Question: What challenge do Catholics give to Protestants concerning Sunday?

Answer: The church changed the observance of the Sabbath to Sunday by rite of the divine, infallible authority given to her by her Founder, Jesus Christ. *The Protestant, claiming the Bible to be the only guide of faith, has no warrant for observing Sunday.* (*Catholic Universe Bulletin,* Aug. 14, 1942)

Q. *Have you any other way of proving that the Church has power to institute festivals of precept?*

A. Had she not such power, she could not have done that in which all modern religionists agree with her:—she could not have substituted the observance of Sunday the first day of the week, for the observance of Saturday the seventh day, a change for which *there is no Scriptural authority.* (Reverend Stephan Keenan, *A Doctrinal Catechism,* 1876, p. 174, available at https://1ref.us/22z, accessed Sept. 22, 2022)

Protestantism, in discarding the authority of the [Roman Catholic] Church, *has no good reason for its Sunday theory,* and ought, logically, to keep Saturday as the Sabbath. (John Gilmary Shea, "The Observance of Sunday and Civil Laws for Its Enforcement," *The American Catholic Quarterly Review,* January 1883, p. 152)

It is well to remind the Presbyterians, Baptists, Methodists, and all other Christians, that the Bible does not support them anywhere in their observance of Sunday. *Sunday is an institution of the Roman Catholic Church, and those who observe the day observe commandment of the Catholic Church.* (Priest Brady, in an address reported in the *Elizabeth, New Jersey News,* March 18, 1903)

> **Reason and common sense** demand the acceptance of one or the other of these alternatives; either *Protestantism and the keeping holy of Saturday,* or Catholicity and the keeping holy of Sunday. Compromise is impossible. (*The Catholic Mirror,* Dec. 23, 1893)
>
> If Protestants would follow the Bible, they should worship God on the Sabbath Day. *In keeping the Sunday, they are following a law of the Catholic Church.* (Albert Smith, Chancellor of the Archdiocese of Baltimore, replying for the Cardinal in a letter dated February 10, 1920)
>
> Protestants ... accept Sunday rather than Saturday as the day for the public worship after the Catholic Church made the change ... But the Protestant mind does not seem to realize that in accepting the Bible, *in observing the Sunday, they are accepting the authority of the spokesman for the church, the Pope.* (*Our Sunday Visitor,* Feb. 5, 1950)
>
> **We have in the authoritative voice of the Church the voice of Christ Himself.** The *Church is above the Bible;* and this transference of Sabbath observance from Saturday to Sunday is proof of that fact. Deny the authority of the Church and you have no adequate or reasonable explanation or justification for the substitution of Sunday for Saturday in the Third—Protestant Fourth—Commandment of God. (*The Catholic Record,* London, Ontario, Sept. 1, 1923)
>
> The chancellor to Cardinal Gibbons wrote in response to a question about changing the
>
> Of course the Catholic Church claims that the change was her act. It could not have been otherwise as none in those days would have dreamed of doing anything in matters spiritual and ecclesiastical and religious without her. And the act is *a mark of her ecclesiastical authority* in religious things. (Letter, C. F. Thomas, chancellor for James Cardinal Gibbons, Nov. 11, 1895, emphasis added)

These Catholic statements prove that God created the seventh-day Sabbath and then the Catholic Church changed it to Sunday. The last Catholic statement informs us that we need to read Revelation 13 which tells us about the *"mark of the beast"* because the last Catholic quotation proves to us that they call their Sunday law their *"mark."*

Revelation 13 explains that, in the last days, one beast power will make those living on the earth follow another beast power and its **mark.** If you look up verses 1 through 10 of the chapter, you will see that the beast power with a mark is the **Roman Catholic Church who have claimed that their Sunday worship law is their mark.**

Then, verses 11 through 18 indicate that the enforcing beast power will force the inhabitants of the earth to follow the Roman Catholic Church's Sunday law, which they themselves call their *mark.* Here is the description:

> And I beheld another beast coming up out of the earth; and he had two horns like a lamb, and he spake as a dragon. [12] And he exerciseth all the power of the first beast before him, and causeth the earth and them which dwell therein to worship the first beast, whose deadly wound was healed. (Rev. 13:11, 12)

Here is the description of the second beast forcing everyone to follow the Roman Catholic Church and receive their *mark.*

> And that no man might buy or sell, save he that had the *mark,* or the name of the beast, or the number of his name. (Rev. 13:17)

This warning tells us why we need to abandon the **Sunday worship** that the Catholic Church created and observe the *holy Sabbath* that *Jesus created* when He created this world. Sunday worship is a ***lie*** about what day we are to worship God. Satan originated lying, and worshiping on Sunday is the greatest lie that Satan has created through the Roman Catholic Church!

Chapter 4

The Sabbath, Is It for Jews or for Gentiles?

Here are God's words about His holy day.

Thus, the heavens and the earth were finished, and all the host of them.² And on the *seventh day* God ended his work which he had made; and he **rested on the seventh day** from all his work which he had made.³ And God **blessed the seventh day and sanctified it:** because that in it he had rested from all his work which God created and made. (Gen. 2:1–3)

If the Sabbath was given to Adam at creation, then it couldn't have been just for the Jews since none existed at the creation of the world.

God blessed a twenty-four-hour period of *time* as His gift of rest to mankind one day each week. He didn't make a holy site like the Muslim **Mecca, the fountainhead and cradle of Islam.** *Time* was something everyone could share every week anywhere in the world. If the Sabbath was **given to Adam** at creation, then it couldn't have been just for the Jews since none existed at the creation of the world. God referred to that rest in Exodus 16.

Six days ye shall gather it; but on the *seventh day,* which is the *Sabbath,* in it there shall be none. ²⁷ And it came to pass, that there went out some of the people on the seventh day for to gather, and they found none. ²⁸ And the LORD said unto Moses, How long refuse ye to keep my commandments and my laws? ²⁹ See, for that the LORD hath given you the Sabbath, therefore he giveth you on the sixth day the bread of two days;

abide ye every man in his place, let no man go out of his place on the seventh day. ³⁰ So the people rested on the seventh day. (Exod. 16:26–30)

So, the LORD asked Moses how long the Jews were going to refuse to keep **His commandments and His laws.** This language tells me that the Sabbath was already one of God's laws—even before He wrote the Ten Commandments for Moses to take from Mount Sinai. For those who claim the Sabbath is only for the Jews, how could this have happened before Moses met Jesus on Mount Sinai when Jesus Himself wrote the Ten Commandments? Also, the Sabbath was required of the mixed multitude who came out of Egypt with the Jews, as we see in the fourth commandment.

Exodus 20:8-11

Remember the Sabbath day, to keep it holy. ⁹ Six days shalt thou labour, and do all thy work: ¹⁰ But the seventh day is the Sabbath of the LORD thy God: in it thou shalt not do any work, thou, nor thy son, nor thy daughter, nor thy manservant, nor thy maidservant, nor thy cattle, nor thy stranger that is within thy gates: ¹¹ For in six days the LORD made heaven and earth, the sea, and all that in them is, and rested the seventh day: wherefore the LORD blessed the Sabbath day, and hallowed it.

If a stranger that is on someone's property has to keep the Sabbath holy, then it cannot have been designed for just the Jews.

Matthew 12:8

For the Son of man is Lord even of the Sabbath day.

If the *Son of Man* is *Lord of the Sabbath,* then the Sabbath must be the Lord's day in which John found himself when he heard a great voice behind him.

Revelation 1:10

I was in the Spirit on the Lord's day, and heard behind me a great voice, as of a trumpet.

Mark 2:27-28

And he said unto them, The Sabbath was made for man, and not man for the Sabbath: ²⁸ Therefore the Son of man is Lord also of the Sabbath.

Jesus did not say that the Sabbath was made for Jews. He said that it was made for *man*. The word "man" (**G444** in *Strong's Concordance*), in the original

Greek language, simply means a human being. That sounds to me like the Sabbath was made for *every living person* in the world and not just for the Jews.

> **Luke 4:16**
>
> And he came to Nazareth, where he had been brought up: and, as *his custom was*, he went into the synagogue on the **Sabbath day,** and stood up for to read.

If someone *follows Christ,* then he or she is a Christian.

The Definition of "Christian"

"A Christian is someone who follows the *teachings* of **Jesus Christ** ..."

If Jesus' custom was to observe the Sabbath, then that tells me that any who is a Christian will follow Jesus and do the same thing in following Him. At least that is what we are told to do by the apostle Peter in the following verse.

> **1 Peter 2:21**
>
> For even hereunto were ye called: because Christ also suffered for us, leaving us an example, that *ye should follow his steps.*

One of *Jesus' steps* was to keep the **Sabbath.**

> **Matthew 24:20**
>
> But pray ye that your flight be not in the winter, neither on the Sabbath day.

In this verse, Jesus was speaking about the coming **destruction** of **Jerusalem in 70 AD.** He apparently thought that His followers would be keeping the Sabbath after His resurrection and **not observing Sunday in honor of His resurrection.** What day was the Sabbath after Jesus died?

> **Luke 23:52-56, 24:1**
>
> This man went unto Pilate, and begged the body of Jesus. [53] And he took it down, and wrapped it in linen, and laid it in a sepulchre that was hewn in stone, wherein never man before was laid. [54] And that day was the preparation, and the Sabbath drew on. [55] And the women also, which came with him from Galilee, followed after, and beheld the sepulchre, and how his body was laid. [56] And they returned, and prepared spices and ointments; and rested the Sabbath day according to the commandment. [1] Now upon the first day of the week, very early

in the morning, they came unto the sepulchre, bringing the spices which they had prepared, and certain others with them.

Here the Scriptures leave **no doubt** about which day was the **Sabbath day.** They delineate three days in succession: **Friday** (or preparation day), then the **Sabbath,** and then the first day of the week, which is **Sunday.** It's interesting that even in Jesus' death, **He kept the Sabbath** by resting.

Acts 13:42-44

And when the Jews were gone out of the synagogue, the Gentiles besought that these words might be preached to them the next Sabbath.[43] Now when the congregation was broken up, many of the Jews and religious proselytes followed Paul and Barnabas: who, speaking to them, persuaded them to continue in the grace of God.[44] And the next Sabbath day came almost the whole city together to hear the word of God.

So, **Paul** kept the Sabbath as well as the **Gentiles** who were converted.

Acts 16:13

And on the Sabbath, we went out of the city by a river side, where prayer was wont to be made; and we sat down, and spake unto the women which resorted thither.

Again, Paul is keeping the Sabbath.

Ezekiel 20:12, 19-21

Moreover, also I gave them my Sabbaths, to be *a sign between me and them,* that they might know that I am the LORD that sanctify them. [19] I am the LORD your God; walk in my statutes, and keep my judgments, and do them; [20] And hallow my Sabbaths; and they shall be a sign between me and you, that ye may know that I am the LORD your God. [21] Notwithstanding the children rebelled against me: they walked not in my statutes, neither kept my judgments to do them, which if a man do, he shall even live in them; they polluted my Sabbaths: then I said, I would pour out my fury upon them, to accomplish my anger against them in the wilderness.

The Sabbath is God's sign that we are sanctified.

Isaiah 56:2, 6, 7

> Blessed is the man that doeth this, and the son of man that layeth hold on it; that keepeth the Sabbath from polluting it, and keepeth his hand from doing any evil. ⁶ Also the sons of the stranger, that join themselves to the LORD, to serve him, and to love the name of the LORD, to be his servants, every one that keepeth the Sabbath from polluting it, and taketh hold of my covenant; ⁷ Even them will I bring to my holy mountain, and make them joyful in my house of prayer: their burnt offerings and their sacrifices shall be accepted upon mine altar; for mine house shall be called an house of prayer for all people.

This tells me that anyone who keeps the *Sabbath* is a **blessed person.** This also tells me that the *Sabbath* is for any "stranger" that becomes a child of Abraham through faith, who will be brought to God's holy mountain for keeping the *Sabbath.*

Isaiah 58:12-14

> And they that shall be of thee shall build the old waste places: thou shalt raise up the foundations of many generations; and thou shalt be called, The repairer of the breach, The restorer of paths to dwell in. ¹³ If thou turn away thy foot from the Sabbath, from doing thy pleasure on my holy day; and call the Sabbath a delight, the holy of the LORD, honourable; and shalt honour him, not doing thine own ways, nor finding thine own pleasure, nor speaking thine own words: ¹⁴ Then shalt thou delight thyself in the LORD; and I will cause thee to ride upon the high places of the earth, and feed thee with the heritage of Jacob thy father: for the mouth of the LORD hath spoken it.

Repairing the breach, or restoring paths, clearly refers to making the observance of the *Sabbath* a priority again.

Isaiah 66:22-23

> For as the new heavens and the new earth, which I will make, shall remain before me, saith the LORD, so shall your seed and your name remain. ²³ And it shall come to pass, that from one new moon to another, and from one Sabbath to another, shall all flesh come to worship before me, saith the LORD.

If any Jew **does not believe that Jesus is the Son of God,** then he or she is not one who will be **keeping the Sabbath in the new earth,** for he or she will not be there.

All of these Bible verses tell me that **God did not create the Sabbath** for the Jews but that He created it for *every living creature* on our planet.

Not only did God create the Sabbath for a day of rest for every living being, but He also is not the one *who changed the Sabbath* to **Sunday** for Christians.

Consider what **Priest Thomas Enright, CSSR,** President of Redemptorist College, Kansas City, Missouri, said in his Hartford, Kansas, lecture on February 18, 1884, as it was printed in the February 22, 1884, *Hartford Kansas Weekly Call:*

> "The Bible says, 'Remember the Sabbath day to keep it holy.' The Catholic Church says, *No.* By my divine power *I abolish the Sabbath day* and *command you to keep holy the first day of the week.* And lo! The entire civilized world bows down in reverent obedience to the command of the Holy Catholic Church."

What **Protestants need to understand** is that, when they accept Sunday as a day of public worship, they are *following the Catholic Church and not Jesus.*

Here is another **Catholic** statement made in *Our Sunday Visitor,* February 5, 1950.

> "Protestants … accept Sunday rather than Saturday as the day for the public worship after the Catholic Church made the change … But the Protestant mind does not seem to realize that *… in observing the Sunday, they are accepting the authority of the spokesman for the church, the Pope."*

According to **Ellen G. White,** God's followers are the ones who need to **oppose those** who changed God's law from the *Sabbath to Sunday.*

> In the very time in which we live, the Lord has called His people and has given them a message to bear. He has called them to expose the wickedness of the man of sin who has made the *Sunday law* a distinctive power, who has thought **to change times and laws,** and to oppress the people of God who stand firmly to honor Him by keeping the only true Sabbath, the Sabbath of creation, as holy unto the Lord. (Ellen G. White, *Testimonies to Ministers,* p. 117)

We have already read in Daniel chapter 7 that the comment, **"to change times and laws,"** is in God's Word, the Bible.

> And he shall speak great words against the most High, and shall wear out the saints of the most High, **and think to change times and laws:** and they shall be given into his hand until a time and times and the dividing of time. (Dan. 7:25)

So, the Bible establishes that the little horn power *(the Roman Catholic Church)* would *"think to change times and laws"* created for Gentiles and not just for the Jews. Also, the Catholic church has *thought* it has changed God's law from the Sabbath to Sunday worship.

Original Languages

As we draw this chapter to a close, one more interesting fact is that the words in the original languages used to designate the seventh day of the week as the "Sabbath" have continued to be very similar while the other names have so changed over time that they are unintelligible to people of other language groups. This is another proof that the Sabbath and the words used to designate the seventh day of the week as the "Sabbath day" originated at Creation in complete harmony with the biblical record found in Genesis 2:1–3.

In the majority of the principal languages the last, or seventh, day of the week is designated as **"*Sabbath.*"** There is not even one language that designates another day as the "day of rest."

I cannot speak firsthand for all of these languages, but I can speak firsthand for the **Gogodala language of Papua New Guinea** where our family served as missionaries from 1997 to 2002. The Gogodala have no names for the days of the week. They have no name for Sunday, Monday, Tuesday, Wednesday, Thursday, or Friday. The only day they have a name for is the seventh day which they call *Sabadi*. To say **"*happy Sabbath*"** in the Gogodala language, you say, "*Sa:lanapa* **Sabadi** *Kadepa.*"

Here is a list of countries that use the name "Sabbath" to describe the seventh day of the week.

Language	7th Day	Meaning
Gogodala of Papua New Guinea	Sabadi	Sabbath
Greek	Sabbaton	Sabbath
Latin (Italy)	Sabbatum	Sabbath
Spanish (Spain)	Sábado	Sabbath
Portuguese (Portugal)	Sabbado	Sabbath
Italian (Italy)	Sabbato	Sabbath
French (France)	Samedi	Sabbath day
High German (Germany)	Samstag	Sabbath
Prussian (Prussia)	Sabatico	Sabbath

Russian (Russia)	Subbota	Sabbath
Polish	Sobota	Sabbath
Afghan	Shamba	Sabbath
Hindustani	Shamba	Sabbath
Persian	Shambin	Sabbath
Turkish	Yomessabt	Day Sabbath
Malay	Hari-Sabtu	Day Sabbath
Abyssinian	Yini Sanbat	Sabbath
Lusatian (Saxony)	Sobota	Sabbath
Bohemian	Sobota	Sabbath
Bulgarian	Sùbbota	Sabbath
New Slovenian	Sobóta	Sabbath
Illyrian	Subota	Sabbath
Wallachian (Roumania)	Sâmbătă	Sabbath
Roman	Dissapte	Day Sabbath
Ecclesiastical Roman	Sabbatum	Sabbath
D'oc. French	Dissata, Dissate	Day Sabbath
Norman French (10th–11th Centuries)	Sabbedi, Samaday, Semadi	Sabbath Day
Wolof (Senegambia, West Africa)	Alere-Asser	Last Day Sabbath
Congo (West Equatorial Africa)	Sabbado	Sabbath
Orma (South of Abyssinia)	Zam-ba-da	Sabbath
Kazani-Tartar (East Russia)	Subbota	Sabbath
Osmanlian (Turkey)	Yom-es-sabt	day of the Sabbath
Ancient Syriac	Shab-ba-tho	Sabbath
Chaldee Syriac (Kurdistan, Urumia, Persia)	Shapta	Sabbath
Babylonian Syriac (a very old language)	Sa-ba-tū	Sabbath
Pahlavi (ancient Persian)	Shambid	Sabbath, pleasantest day of week
Persian (Persia)	Shambah	Sabbath

Armenian (Armenia)	Shapat	Sabbath
Kurdish (Kurdistan)	Shamba	Sabbath
Ndebele (Zimbabwe)	Sabatha	Sabbath
Shona (Zimbabwe)	Sabata	Sabbath
Georgian (Caucasus)	Shabati	Sabbath
Suanian (Caucasus)	Sammtyn	Sabbath
Ingoush (Caucasus)	Shatt	Sabbath
Malayan (Malaya, Sumatra)	Hari sabtū	day Sabbath
Javanese (Java)	Saptoe	Sabbath
Dayak (Borneo)	Sabtū	Sabbath
Makssar (southern Celebes and Salayer Islands)	Sattū	Sabbath
Malagassy (Madagascar)	Alsabotsy	The Sabbath
Swahili (east equatorial Africa)	As-sabt	The Sabbath
Mandingo (west Africa, south of Senegal)	Sibiti	Sabbath
Teda (central Africa)	Essébdu	The Sabbath
Bornu (central Africa)	Sibda	The Sabbath
Lógonē (central Africa)	Se'-sibde	The Sabbath
Bágrimma (central Africa)	Sibbedī	Sabbath
Maba (central Africa)	Sab	Sabbath
Permian (Russian)	Suböta	Sabbath
Votiak (Russian)	Subbota	Sabbath
Shemitic Hebrew Bible world-wide	Yom ha-shab-bath	Day the Sabbath
Hebrew (Ancient and Modern)	Shab-bath	Sabbath
Targum of Onkelos (Hebrew Literature)	Yom ha-shab-bath	Day the Sabbath
Targum Dialect of the Jews in Kurdistan	yoy-met sha-bat kodesh	Holy Sabbath Day
Ancient Syriac	Shab-ba-tho	Sabbath
Samaritan (Old Hebrew Letters) Palestine	Shab-bath	Sabbath
Babylonian Euphrates Tigris Valleys (3800 B.C.)	Sa-ba-tu	Sabbath
Assyrian Euphrates and Tigris Valleys	sa-ba-tu	Sabbath
Arabic (very old names)	Shĭ-yār	Chief or rejoicing Day

Language	Word	Meaning
Arabic (Ancient and Modern) E,W & N. Africa	as-sabt	The Sabbath
Maltese (Malta)	Is-sibt	The Sabbath
Ge-ez or Ethiopic (Abyssinia)	San-bat	Sabbath
Tigre Abyssinia (closely related to Ge-ez)	San-bat	Sabbath
Amharic, Abyssinia (nearly related to Ge-ez)	san-bat	Sabbath
Falasha (Language of the Jews of Abyssinia)	yini sanbat	The Sabbath
Coptic, Egypt (a language dead for 200 years)	Pī sabbaton	The Sabbath
Tamashek or Towarek (Atlas mountains, Africa)	A-hal es-sabt	The Sabbath
Kabyle or Berber. (North Africa, Ancient Numidian)	Ghas or wass assebt	The Sabbath Day
Hausa (Central Africa)	Assebatū	the Sabbath
Pashto or Afghan Afghanistan	uses the word "Sabbath" in describing every day of the week	
Pashto or Afghan Afghanistan		One to the Sabbath
Pashto or Afghan Afghanistan		Two to Sabbath
Pashto or Afghan Afghanistan		Three to Sabbath
Pashto or Afghan Afghanistan		Four to Sabbath
Pashto or Afghan Afghanistan		Assembly (day)
Pashto or Afghan Afghanistan	khali, Shamba	unemployed-day, Sabbath

This is another reason I believe that the Sabbath was **not created for the Jews only** but for the **entire world** and that God wants us all to keep it holy.

Chapter 5

A Significant Catholic Document

Below is a document that was written in 1869 by the *Roman Catholic Church* addressing *Protestants* outside the Roman Catholic Church. I have added boldfacing, italics, and color to emphasize the main words I want you to recognize. Other than this formatting, every word in this chapter is from the original document. After the document, I will add some comments. Here is the document:

Why don't you keep holy the Sabbath-day?

Why do you not keep holy the Sabbath-day?

I am going to propose a very plain and serious question, to which I would entreat all who profess to follow **"the Bible and the Bible only"** to give their most earnest attention. It is this: *Why do you not keep holy the Sabbath-day?*

The command of Almighty God stands **clearly written** in the Bible in these words: "**Remember the Sabbath-day,** to keep it holy. Six days shalt thou labour, and do all thy work; but the seventh day is the Sabbath of the Lord thy God; in it thou shalt not do any work" (Exod. xx. 8–10). And again, "Six days shall work be done; but on the seventh day there shall be to you an holy day, a Sabbath of rest to the Lord; whosoever doeth work therein shall be put to death. Ye shall kindle no fire throughout your habitations upon the Sabbath-day" (Exod. xxxv. 2, 3).

How strict and precise is God's commandment upon this head! [in this matter!] No work whatever was to be done on the day which He had chosen to set apart for Himself and to make holy; He required of His people that they should not even light a fire upon that day. And accordingly, when the children of Israel "found a man that gathered sticks upon the Sabbath-day" "the Lord said unto Moses, The man shall be surely put to death; all the congregation shall stone him with stones without the camp" (Numbers xv. 35). Such being God's command then, I ask again, Why do you not obey it? *Why do you not keep holy the Sabbath-day?*

You will answer me, perhaps, that you do keep holy the Sabbath-day; for that you abstain from all worldly business, and diligently go to church, and say your prayers, and read your Bible at home, every Sunday of your lives.

But Sunday is not the Sabbath-day. *Sunday is the first day of the week*; **the Sabbath-day was the seventh day of the week.** Almighty God did not give a commandment that men should keep holy one day in seven; but He named His own day, and said distinctly, "Thou shalt keep holy the *seventh day;*" and He assigned a reason for choosing this day rather than any other—a reason which belongs only to the seventh day of the week, and **cannot be applied to the rest.** He says, "For in six days the Lord made heaven and earth, the sea and all that in them is, and rested the seventh day; wherefore the Lord blessed the Sabbath-day and hallowed it." [Exodus xx. 11.]

Almighty God ordered that all men should rest from their labour on the seventh day, because He too had rested on that day: He did not rest on Sunday, but on Saturday. **On Sunday, which is the first day of the week, He** began **the work of creation, He did not finish it [then]; it was on Saturday that He "ended His work which He had made; and He rested on the seventh day from all His work which He had made; and God blessed the seventh day, and sanctified it, because that in it He had rested from all His work which God created and made"** (Gen. ii. 2, 3). Nothing can be more plain and easy to understand than all this; and there is nobody who attempts to deny it; it is acknowledged by every body that the day which Almighty God appointed to be kept holy was Saturday, not Sunday. *Why then do you keep holy the Sunday, and not Saturday?*

You will tell me that Saturday was the Jewish Sabbath [though God gave the Bible Sabbath to mankind 2,000 years before the first Jew existed], but that the Christian Sabbath has been changed to Sunday; changed! **but by whom?** Who has authority to change an express commandment of Almighty God? When God has spoken and said, Thou shalt keep holy the seventh day, who shall dare to say, Nay, thou mayest work and do all manner of worldly business on the seventh day; but thou shalt keep holy the first day in its stead? ***This is a most important question, which I know not how you can answer.***

You are a Protestant, and you profess to go by the Bible and the Bible only; and yet in so important a matter as the observance of one day in seven as a holy day, you go against the plain letter of the Bible, and put another day in the place of that day which the Bible had commanded. ***The command to keep holy the seventh day is one of the ten commandments;*** you believe that the *other nine* are still binding; who gave you authority to tamper with the fourth? If you are consistent with your own principles, if you really follow the Bible and the Bible only, you ought to be able to produce some portion of the New Testament in which this fourth commandment is expressly altered, or at least from which you may confidently infer that it was the will of God that Christians should make that change in its observance which you have made.

Let us see whether any such passages can be found. I will look for them in the writings of your own [Protestant] champions, who have attempted to defend your practice in this matter.

1. The first text which I find quoted upon the subject is this: "Let no man judge you in respect of an holy day, or of the new moon, or of the Sabbath-days" (Col. ii. 16). [That refers to the ceremonial—sacrificial—yearly sabbaths of Leviticus 23, which were done away at the cross.] I could understand a Bible Christian arguing from this passage, that we ought to make no difference between Saturday, Sunday, and every other day of the week; that under the Christian dispensation all such distinctions of days were done away with; one day was as good and as holy as another; there were to be no Sabbaths, no holy days at all. But not one syllable does it say about the obligation of the Sabbath being transferred from one day to another.

2. Secondly, the words of St. John are quoted, "I was in the Spirit on the Lord's day" (Apoc. [Revelation] i. 10). Is it possible that any body can for a moment imagine that here is a safe and clear rule for changing the weekly feast from the seventh to the first day? This passage is utterly silent upon such a subject; it does but give us scriptural authority for calling some one day in particular (it does not even say which day) "the Lord's day."

3. Next we are reminded that St. Paul bade his Corinthian converts, "upon the first day of the week, lay by them in store, that there might be no gatherings" when he himself came (1 Cor. xvi. 2). How is this supposed to affect the law of the Jewish Sabbath? It commands a certain act of almsgiving [doing one's finances at home] to be done on the first day of the week. It says absolutely nothing about not doing certain other acts of prayer and public worship on the seventh day.

4. But [you will say] it was "on the first day of the week" when the disciples were assembled with closed doors for fear of the Jews, and Jesus stood in the midst of them; and again, it was eight days afterwards (that is, on the first day of the following week) that "the disciples were within, and Thomas with them," and Jesus again came and stood in the midst (John xx. 19, 26): that is to say, it was on the evening of the day of the Resurrection that our Lord first shewed Himself to many disciples gathered together; and after eight days He again shewed Himself to the same company, with the further addition of St. Thomas. What is there in these facts to do away with the obligation of keeping holy the seventh day? Our Lord rose from the dead on the first day of the week, and on the same day at evening He appears to many of His disciples; He appears again on that day [of the] week, and perhaps also on other days in the interval. Let Protestants, if they will [in obedience to Catholic tradition], keep holy the first day of the week in grateful commemoration of that stupendous mystery, the Resurrection of Christ, and of the evidences which He vouchsafed to give of it to His doubting disciples; but this is no scriptural authority for ceasing to keep holy another day of the week which God had expressly commanded to be kept holy for another and altogether different reason.

5. But lastly, we have the example of the Apostles themselves. "Upon the first day of the week, when the disciples came together to break bread, Paul preached unto them, ready to depart on the morrow; and continued his speech until midnight" (Acts xx. 7). Here we have clear proof that the disciples came together for the celebration of the Holy Eucharist, and that they heard a sermon on a Sunday. But is there any proof that they had not done the same on the Saturday also? Is it not expressly written concerning those early Christians, that they "continued daily with one accord in the

temple, breaking bread from house to house?" (Acts ii. 46.) And as a matter of fact, do we not know from other sources that, in many parts of the Church, the ancient Christians were in the habit of meeting together for public worship, to receive Holy Communion, and to perform the other [religious] offices, on Saturdays just the same as on Sundays? Again, then, I say, [in obedience to our command] let Protestants keep holy, if they will, the first day of the week, in order that they may resemble those Christians who were gathered together on that day in an upper chamber in Troas; but let them remember that this cannot possibly release them from the obligation of keeping holy another day which Almighty God has ordered to be kept holy, because on that day He "rested from all His work." [The Troas meeting was held on Sunday in Acts 20:7, just prior to a Miletus meeting on Tuesday in Acts 20:17–38, although no one today keeps Tuesday sacred because of that meeting.]

[Acts xiii. 14, 42–44; xvi. 12, 13; xvii. 1, 2; xviiii. 1–4, 11; after the night meeting on the first day in Troas (Acts xx. 7), Paul held a meeting on Tuesday in Miletus (Acts xx. 17–38). But no one considers that meeting sacred.]

I do not know of any other passages of holy Scripture which Protestants are in the habit of quoting to defend their practice of keeping holy the first day of the week instead of the seventh; yet surely those which I have quoted are not such as should satisfy any reasonable man, who looks upon the written word of God as they [the Protestants] profess to look upon it, namely, as the one only appointed means of learning God's will, and who really desires to learn and to obey that will in all things with humbleness and simplicity of heart. It is absolutely impossible that a reasonable and thoughtful person should be satisfied, by the texts that I have quoted, that Almighty God intended the obligation of Saturday under the old law to be transferred to Sunday under the new. And yet Protestants do so transfer it, and never seem to have the slightest misgivings lest, in doing so, they should be guilty of breaking one of God's commandments.

Why is this? Because, although they talk so largely about following the Bible and the Bible only, they are really guided in this matter by the voice of *[Roman Catholic] tradition.* Yes, much as they may hate and denounce the word [tradition], they have in fact no other authority to allege for this most important change.

The present generation of Protestants keep Sunday holy instead of Saturday, because they received it as part of the Christian religion from the last generation, and that generation received it from the generation before, and so on backwards from one generation to another, by a continual succession, until we come to the time of the (so-called) Reformation, when it so happened that those who conducted the change of religion in this country [from Catholicism to Protestantism] left this particular portion of Catholic faith and practice untouched.

But, had it happened otherwise,—had some one or other of the "Reformers" taken it into his head to denounce the observance of Sunday as a Popish corruption and superstition, and to insist upon it that Saturday was the day which God had appointed to be kept holy, and that He had never authorised the observance of any other,—all Protestants would have been obliged, in obedience to their professed principle of following **the Bible and the Bible only,** either to acknowledge this teaching as true, and to return to the observance of the ancient Jewish Sabbath, or else to deny that there is any Sabbath at all. And so, in like manner, any one at the present day who should set about, honestly and without prejudice, to draw up for himself a form of religious belief and practice out of the written Word of God, must needs come to the same conclusion: **he must either believe that the Jewish [biblical seventh-day] Sabbath is still binding upon men's consciences, because of the Divine command, "Thou shalt keep holy the seventh day;" or he must believe that no Sabbath at all is binding upon them, because of the Apostolic injunction, "Let no man judge you in respect of a festival day, or of the Sabbaths, which are a shadow of things to come, but the body is Christ's."** [Paul would have no right to abolish any of the Ten Commandments.] Either one or the other of these conclusions he might honestly come to; but he would know nothing whatever of a Christian Sabbath distinct from the Jewish [biblical Sabbath], celebrated on a different day, and observed in a different manner, simply because holy Scripture itself nowhere speaks of such a thing.

Now, mind, in all this you would greatly misunderstand me if you supposed I was quarrelling with you for acting in this matter on a true and right principle, in other words, a Catholic principle; viz. the acceptance, without hesitation, of that which has been handed down to you by an unbroken tradition. I would not tear from you a single one of those shreds and fragments of Divine truth [Catholic truth] which you have retained. God forbid! They are the most precious things you possess, and by God's blessing may serve as clues to bring you out of that labyrinth of [Protestant] error in which you find yourselves involved, far more by the fault of your forefathers three centuries ago [when they left Rome during the sixteenth-century Reformation] than by your own.

What I do quarrel with you for is, not your inconsistency in occasionally acting on a true principle [such as Roman Catholic Sunday keeping], but your adoption, as a general rule, of a false one [your Protestant refusal to accept the rest of Roman traditional teachings; such as the Mass and the veneration of saints]. You keep the Sunday, and not the Saturday; and you do so rightly, for this was the practice of all Christians when Protestantism began [Catholic leaders erroneously say there were no Protestants prior to the sixteenth century]; but you have abandoned other Catholic observances which were equally universal at that day, preferring the novelties introduced by the men who invented Protestantism, to the unvarying tradition of above 1500 years [of Catholic teaching]. **We blame you not for making Sunday your weekly holy-day instead of Saturday, but for** *rejecting tradition* **[the sayings of the popes and councils of Rome], which is the** *only safe and clear rule* **by which this** *observance [of Sunday]* **can be justified.**

In outward act we do the same as yourselves in this matter; we too no longer observe the Jewish Sabbath, but Sunday in its stead; but then there is this important difference between us, that *we do not pretend*, as you do, to derive our authority for so doing from a book [the Bible], but we [Catholics] derive it from a ***living teacher,*** and that teacher is the ***[Roman Catholic] Church.*** Moreover, we believe that not every thing which God would have us to know and to do is written in the Bible, but that there is also an unwritten word of God [the sayings of **popes and councils** and canonized saints], which *we* are bound to *believe and to obey*, just as we believe and obey the Bible itself, according to that saying of the Apostle, "Stand fast and hold the traditions which you have learned, whether by word or by our epistle" (2 Thess. ii. 14).

We Catholics, then, have precisely the same authority for keeping Sunday holy instead of Saturday as we have for every other article of our creed, namely, **the authority of "the Church of the living God, the pillar and ground of the truth"** (1 Tim. iii. 15); whereas you who are Protestants have really no authority for it [Sunday sacredness] whatever; *for there is no authority for it in the Bible,* and you will not allow that there can be authority for it any where else. ***Both you and we do, in fact, follow [Catholic] tradition in this matter;*** but we follow it, believing it to be a part of God's word, and the [Catholic] Church to be its divinely-appointed guardian and interpreter; ***you follow it*** [Catholicism], denouncing it all the time as a fallible and treacherous guide, which often "makes the commandment of God of none effect." [Matt. xv. 6.]

"Why Don't You Keep Holy the Sabbath Day?" *The Clifton Tracts,* vol. 4, London: Burns and Lambert, 1852, pp. 3–15, published by the Roman Catholic Church; released in North America, through the T. W. Strong Publishing Company of New York City, in 1869, so those outside the papal fold may fully return under the authority of the Mother Church of the Vatican, available at https://1ref.us/230, accessed Sept. 22, 2022.

Here are my comments:

So, the Roman Catholic Church is ***frustrated*** with *Protestants* because they will not follow *all of* the Catholic Church's ***traditions*** that they want Protestants to follow, even though Protestants are worshiping on **Sunday,** one of the **Catholic Church's** traditions, rather than *God's law,* which they claim to be following!

This letter, written in 1852, was penned to convince those who keep *Sunday* as a worship day to become Catholics because they *are* keeping one of their traditions, **Sunday worship.**

Yet, God proclaims, in John 14:15, "If ye love me, keep my commandments."

And God's fourth commandment says to "Remember the Sabbath day to keep it Holy," so that is what God actually wants us to do!

Chapter 6

What is the "Truth" about the Mark of the Beast?

WARNING: The *devil* does not want you to study the *"truth"* about the **Mark of the Beast.** The Mark of the Beast is one of the most lied about prophecies in all of the Bible, yet it is a prophecy we must understand. God loves His people and wants them to know the *truth.* This message is not from me; it comes from Jesus. And with eternal death facing those who **receive the mark,** it would be wrong to not help Jesus deliver this message.

Lucifer, who invented lying and became known as **Satan,** after being cast out of heaven, amazingly has won the support of the majority of earth's people in his rebellion. Soon every living person on this earth will have aligned with either **Satan or** *with* **God.** The final battle between Satan and God is described in the book of Revelation. This prophetic book points out that God has a **mark** that will identify His people and that Satan also has a **mark** that will identify those who support him. As usual, Satan will use an earthly power, symbolized in Revelation by a beast, to impose his mark. This paper has been written to reveal the **beast's mark.**

Let's begin by identifying **the beast in Revelation 13:1–8.**

Revelation 13:1–8

"And I stood upon the sand of the sea, and saw a **beast rise up out of the sea,** having **seven heads** and **ten horns,** and upon his horns **ten crowns,** and upon his heads the name of **blasphemy.** ² And the beast which I saw was like unto a **leopard,** and his feet were as the feet of a **bear,** and his mouth as the mouth of a **lion:** and the dragon gave him his power, and his seat, and great authority. ³ And I saw one of his heads **as it were wounded to death;** and his deadly wound *was healed:* and all the world wondered after the beast. ⁴ And they worshipped the dragon which gave power unto the beast: and they worshipped the beast, saying, Who is like unto the beast? who is able to make war with him? ⁵ And there was given unto him a mouth speaking great things and blasphemies; and power was given unto him to continue forty and two months. ⁶ And he opened his mouth in blasphemy against God, to blaspheme his name, and his tabernacle, and them that dwell in heaven. ⁷ And it was given unto him to make war with the saints, and to overcome them: and power was given him over all kindreds, and tongues, and nations. ⁸ And all that dwell upon the earth shall worship him, whose names are not written in **the book of life** of the Lamb slain from the foundation of the world."

Here are the identifying marks of the beast found in Revelation 13.

Here is one more identification of the **beast.**

Revelation 13:18, BBE

"Here is wisdom. He who has knowledge let him get **the number of the beast;** because it is the number of a man: and his number is **Six hundred and sixty-six.**"

Here are the **identifying marks** of the beast found in Revelation 13.

1. It rises from the sea (verse 1).
2. It is the composite of the four beasts in Daniel chapter 7 (verse 2).
3. The dragon gives it its power and authority (verse 2).
4. It receives a deadly wound (verse 3).
5. Its deadly wound is healed (verse 3).
6. It is a strong political power (verses 3, 7).
7. It is a strong religious power (verses 3, 8).
8. It is guilty of blasphemy (verses 1, 5, 6).
9. It wars with and overcomes the saints (verse 7).
10. It rules for 42 months (verse 5).
11. It has a mysterious number—666 (verse 18).

Do some of these identifying points sound familiar? They should! If you have studied **Daniel 7** about the **Antichrist,** then you have already learned that the **little horn power (Antichrist) was the** *papacy.* The "beast" introduced in **Revelation 13:1** is simply another name for the **"Antichrist,"** or the *papacy.* If we study Daniel and Revelation together, we will find that both books identify beasts in Bible prophecies, adding additional details that establish an accurate interpretation. In studying **Revelation 13,** we will learn some new things about the **Antichrist.** Let us now consider, one by one, the 11 points that describe the beast.

1. It would rise from the sea (Revelation 13:1).

The sea (or water) in prophecy refers to people or a populated area (see Rev. 17:15). So, the beast known as the Antichrist had to arise amid the established nations of the then known world. The **papacy arose in Western Europe,** so it fits point #1.

2. It would be a composite of the four beasts of Daniel 7 (compare Rev. 13:2).

The four beasts of Daniel 7 are depicted as part of Antichrist, or the beast, because the papacy incorporated pagan beliefs and practices from all four empires. She clothed them in spiritual garb and spread them to the world as Christian teachings.

	The Four Beasts	
	Daniel 7	Revelation 13
Babylon	**Lion**-like beast (v. 4)	Mouth of a **lion** (v. 2)
Medo-Persia	**Bear**-like beast (v. 5)	Feet of a **bear** (v. 2)
Greece	**Leopard**-like beast (v. 6)	Like unto a **leopard** (v. 2)
Rome	**Ten-horned** beast (v. 7)	Having … **ten horns** (v. 1)

Here is one of many supporting statements from history: "In a certain respect, she [the papacy] has ***copied her organization from that of the Roman Empire,*** has preserved and made fruitful the philosophical intuitions of Socrates, Plato and Aristotle, borrowed from both Barbarians and the Byzantine Roman Empire, but always remains herself, thoroughly digesting all elements drawn from external sources" (André Rétif, *The Catholic Spirit,* trans. by Dom Aldhelm Dean, New York, Hawthorne Books, 1959, p. 85, available at https://1ref.us/232, accessed Sept. 22, 2022). This point definitely fits the papacy.

3. The beast must receive its power, seat (capital), and authority from the dragon (Revelation 13:2).

To identify the dragon, we go to **Revelation chapter 12,** where God's end-time church is pictured as a pure woman. In prophecy, a pure woman represents God's true people, or church (Jer. 6:2; Isa. 51:16). The pure woman is portrayed as pregnant and about to deliver a baby. The dragon crouches nearby, hoping to "devour" the baby at birth.

However, when the baby is born, He evades the dragon, fulfills His mission, and then ascends to heaven. Obviously, the baby is **Jesus,** whom Herod tried to destroy by killing all the babies in Bethlehem (Matt. 2:16). So, the **dragon represents pagan Rome,** of which Herod was a king. The power behind Herod's plot was, of course, the devil (Rev. 12:7–9). Satan acts through various governments to accomplish his ugly work. In this case, it was through pagan Rome. Thus, the papacy received her capital city and power from **pagan Rome.**

Here is a historical quotation that supports this statement.

> The mighty Catholic Church was little more than the Roman Empire baptised. Rome was transformed as well as converted. The very capital of the old Empire became the capital of the Christian Empire. The office of Pontifex Maximus was continued in that of Pope. (Alexander Clarence Flick, *The Rise of the Mediaeval Church*, reprint, New York, Burt Franklin, 1959, pp. 148, 149, available at https://1ref.us/231, accessed Sept. 22, 2022)

4. It would receive a deadly wound (Revelation 13:3).

The deadly wound to the papacy was inflicted when **Napoleon's** general, Alexander Berthier, entered Rome and took **Pope Pius VI** captive in February of 1798. **Napoleon** decreed that, at the death of the pope, **the papacy would be discontinued.** The pope died in France in August of 1799. "Half Europe thought ... that without the Pope, the Papacy was dead" (Joseph Rickaby, "The Modern Papacy," *Lectures on the History of Religion,* Lecture 24, London: Catholic Truth Society, 1910, p. 1). So, #4 also fits the papacy.

5. The deadly wound would be healed, and the entire world would give homage to the beast (Revelation 13:3).

This verse states that the deadly wound would heal. Since its healing, the strength of the papacy **has grown.** Today she is one of the most powerful religious-political organizations and influence centers in the world. On Thursday, September 24, 2015, for the first time in history, Pope Francis spoke to the joint session of the United States Congress. If that does not represent a state of power, then nothing does.

ABOUT THE PAPACY:

An American ambassador has said the Vatican is unmatched as a "listening post" (Malachi Martin, *The Keys of This Blood,* New York, Simon & Schuster, 1990, p. 282).

The Papacy is already prepared for worldwide control. Clearly, the wound is healing as the eyes of the nations are upon the Vatican, proving Bible prophecy.

6. It would become a strong political power (Rev. 13:3, 7).

See item 5 above.

7. It would become a very powerful religious organization (Rev. 13:3, 8).

See item 5 above.

8. It would be guilty of blasphemy (Rev. 13:5, 6).

The papacy is guilty of **blasphemy** because her priests claim to **forgive sins** and her popes claim **to be Christ.**

Here is a **Catholic statement** that you have already read that not only proves that they believe they can forgive sinners but that they also claim that even Jesus has to abide by the pope's decision.

> God Himself is obliged to abide by the judgment of His priest, and either not to pardon or to pardon, according as they refuse or give absolution … The sentence of the priest precedes, and *God subscribes to it.* (Alfonso Maria de Saint Liguori, *Dignity and Duties of the Priest,* 1888, p. 27, available at https://1ref.us/22y, accessed Sept. 22, 2022)

Here is a Catholic statement that you also have already read that claims the pope is actually Jesus.

> The Pope is not only the representative of Jesus Christ, but *he is Jesus Christ Himself,* hidden under veil of flesh. (Cardinal Joseph Melchiorre Sarto, *Le Catholique National,* July 13, 1895)

9. It would war with and persecute the saints (Revelation 13:7).

As mentioned in the truth about the Antichrist, the Roman Catholic Church killed an estimated 50 million people during the middle ages.

10. It would reign for 42 months (Revelation 13:5).

The papacy reigned for 42 prophetic months, which equals 1,260 years, from A.D. 538–1798.

11. It would have the mysterious number 666 (Revelation 13:18).

This verse says, "It is the number of a man," and Revelation 15:2 refers to "the number of his name." What man do you think of when you think of the papacy?

Naturally, you think of the pope. **What is his official name?** Here is a Catholic statement to answer that question: "The title of the pope of **Rome is Vicarius Filii Dei** [English: "Vicar of the Son of God"]" ("Answers to Readers' Questions," *Our Sunday Visitor,* Nov. 15, 1914).

Malachi Martin, on page 114 of *The Keys of This Blood,* uses the same title for the pope, "Christ's Vicar on Earth." A footnote for Revelation 13:18 in some Douay versions of the Bible says, "The numeral letters of his name shall make up this number."

V = 5	F = no value	D = 500
I = 1	I = 1	E = no value
C = 100	L = 50	I = 1
A = no value	I = 1	_____
R = no value	I = 1	501
I = 1	_____	
U = 5	53	
S = no value		
_____		
112		112 + 53 + 501 = 666

Roman Numerals: *I = 1, V = 5, X = 10, L = 50, C = 100, D = 500, M = 1000*

This diagram shows what happens when we total up the Roman numeral value of the letters of the name *Vicarius Filii Dei.* There are other names that total up 666 as well, but **no other power in history** could possibly fit **all eleven** divine descriptive points, including the Roman numeral value of its official designation. Now that we can see that the papacy fits all eleven points, we can discover **her mark,** or symbol of authority. But first, by contrast, let's look at **God's sign of authority.**

What is **God's mark,** or symbol, of authority?

It appears to be the *seventh-day Sabbath.* In **Ezekiel 20:12,** Jesus says, "I also gave them My Sabbaths, **to be a *sign*** between them and Me, that they might know that I am the Lord **who sanctifies them."**

Then, in **Exodus 31:17,** He says, "It is a *sign* between Me and the children of Israel **forever;** for in six days the Lord made the heavens and the earth."

In these texts, Jesus is saying that He gave us **His Sabbath** *as a sign* of His power to create and His power to sanctify (convert and save) us. In the Bible, the words **"seal," "sign," "mark,"** and **"token"** are used interchangeably. God's sign, the Sabbath, represents His holy power to rule as Creator and Savior.

In **Hebrews 10:16,** it says that God will put His laws in our hearts and minds.

> This is the covenant that I will make with them after those days, saith the Lord, I will put my laws into their **hearts,** and in their **minds** will I write them. (Heb. 10:16)

Hebrews 4:4–10 confirms this by saying that, when we enter His rest (receive salvation), **we should keep His seventh-day Sabbath holy** as a symbol, or *mark,* of salvation. True Sabbath keeping signifies that a person has surrendered his life to Jesus Christ and is willing to follow wherever Jesus leads.

> For he spake in a certain place of the **seventh day** on this wise, And God did rest the seventh day from all his works. ⁵ And in this place again, If they **shall enter into my rest.** ⁶ Seeing therefore it remaineth that some must enter therein, and they to whom it was first preached entered not in because of unbelief: ⁷ Again, he limiteth a certain day, saying in David, To day, after so long a time; as it is said, To day if ye will hear his voice, harden not your hearts. ⁸ For if Jesus had given them rest, then would he not afterward have spoken of another day. ⁹ There remaineth therefore a rest to the people of God. ¹⁰ For he that is entered into his rest, he also hath ceased from his own works, as God did from his. (Heb. 4:4–10)

Here are two verses that compare **God's mark** on our foreheads.

> Saying, Hurt not the earth, neither the sea, nor the trees, till we have sealed the servants of our God in their **foreheads.** (Rev. 7:3)

> And the LORD said unto him, Go through the midst of the city, through the midst of Jerusalem, and **set a mark** upon the **foreheads** of the men that sigh and that cry for all the abominations that be done in the midst thereof. (Ezek. 9:4)

What does the **papacy** say is her symbol, **or mark,** of authority?

Here again is the answer directly from a Catholic statement:

> Q. Have you any other way of proving that the Church has power to institute festivals of precept?

> A. Had she not such power, she could not have done that in which all modern religionists agree with her:—she could not have substituted the observance of **Sunday** the first day of the week, for the observance of Saturday the seventh day, a change for which there is **no Scriptural authority.** (Stephen Keenan, *A Doctrinal Catechism,* 1876, p. 174)

The papacy is here saying that it "changed" God's holy day from **Sabbath to Sunday** and that virtually all churches accepted the new holy day. Thus, the papacy claims that Sunday as a holy day is **the mark,** or symbol, of her power and authority.

Here again is a Catholic statement in which Catholics claim their Sunday law is **their mark!**

> Of course the Catholic Church claims that the change was her act, ... and the act is a **mark** of her ecclesiastical power. (*H. F. Thomas,* chancellor for James Cardinal Gibbons, Nov. 11, 1895)

> 36. *The Sunday assembly* is the privileged place of unity: it is the setting for the celebration of the *sacramentum unitatis* which profoundly **marks** the Church as a people gathered "by" and "in" the unity of the Father, of the Son and of the Holy Spirit. (Pope John Paul II, *Dies Domini,* May 31, 1998)

Did **God predict** that someone would attempt to change some of His laws?

Daniel 7:25 answers that question.

> And he shall speak great words against the most High, and shall wear out the saints of the most High, **and think to change times and laws:** and they shall be given into his hand until a time and times and the dividing of time. (Dan. 7:25)

To attempt to change God's time, the papacy did two things. They **eliminated the Sabbath,** which is the seventh day of the week, and they **switched it to Sunday** the first day.

Then they changed the daily timing from Sabbath day starting from **Friday night sundown** to **Saturday night sundown** as God created it to **midnight Saturday** night to **midnight Sunday** night.

Here is proof again of what they did from the Catholic catechism:

> The Bible says, remember that thou keep holy the Sabbath day. The Catholic Church says, *No!* By my divine power *I abolish the Sabbath day,* and *command you to keep holy the first day of the week.* And, lo! The entire civilized world bows down in reverent obedience to

the command of the holy Catholic Church. (Father Thomas Enright, President of Redemptorist College, Kansas City, Missouri, Feb. 18, 1884)

God simply gave His [Catholic] Church the power to set aside whatever day or days, she would deem suitable as Holy Days. *The Church chose Sunday,* the first day of the week, and in the course of time added other days, as holy days. (Vincent J. Kelly, *Forbidding Sunday and Feast-day Occupations,* p. 2)

Question: What **challenge** do Catholics give to **Protestants** concerning Sunday?

Catholic Answer:

The Church changed the observance of the Sabbath to Sunday by right of the divine, infallible authority given to her by her Founder, Jesus Christ. *The Protestant, claiming the Bible to be the only guide of faith, has no warrant for observing Sunday.* (*The Catholic Universe Bulletin,* Aug. 14, 1942, p. 4)

Question: Have you any other way of proving that the Church has power to institute festivals of precept?

Catholic Answer:

"Had she not such power, she could not have done that in which all modern religionists agree with her;—she could not have substituted the observance of Sunday the first day of the week, for the observance of Saturday the seventh day, a change for which *there is no Scriptural authority*" (Reverend Stephan Keenan, **A Doctrinal Catechism,** 1848, p. 174, available at https://1ref.us/233, accessed Sept. 22, 2022).

Revelation 13:16 says, "And he causeth all, both small and great, rich and poor, free and bond, to ***receive a mark*** in their ***right hand,*** or in their ***foreheads.***"

This tells us that what we believe in ***our mind*** is the ***mark*** in our forehead and that what we do physically is a ***mark*** in our ***right hand.***

Here is a message that ***God had written*** in the Bible for us in the last days of this earth.

If you keep the Sabbath with care, not doing your business on my holy day; and if the Sabbath seems to you a delight, and the new moon of the Lord a thing to be honoured; and if you give respect to him by not doing your business, or going after your pleasure, or saying unholy words; [14] Then the Lord will be your delight; and I will put you on the high places of the earth; and I will give you the heritage of Jacob your father: for the mouth of the Lord has said it. (Isa. 58:13, 14, BBE)

So, God is asking us to **quit breaking the Sabbath** so He can bless us.

> And the third angel followed them, saying with a loud voice, If any man worship the beast and his image, and **receive his mark** in his forehead, or in his hand, ¹⁰ the same shall drink of the wine of the wrath of God, which is poured out without mixture into the cup of his indignation; and he shall be **tormented with fire** and brimstone in the presence of the holy angels, and in the presence of the Lamb: ¹¹ And the smoke of their torment ascendeth up for ever and ever: and they have no rest day nor night, who worship the beast and his image, and whosoever receiveth the **mark** of his name. ¹² Here is the patience of the saints: here are they that keep the **commandments of God,** and the faith of Jesus. (Revelation 14:9–12)

According to the book of Revelation, **who did John see** in God's eternal kingdom?

> And *I saw* as it were a sea of glass mingled with fire: and them that had gotten the victory over the beast, and over his image, and **over his mark,** and over the number of his name, stand on the sea of glass, having the harps of God. (Revelation 15:2)

So, John sees, in heaven, people **who have God's mark** (the Sabbath) on their foreheads and who **do not have the beast's mark** (Sunday worship).

The Catholic Church actually acknowledges that there is **no** Bible verse that agrees with the *Sunday law.*

> You may read the Bible from Genesis to Revelation, and you will **not find** a single line authorizing the sanctification of Sunday. The Scriptures enforce the religious observance of Saturday, a day which we [Catholics] never sanctify. (James Cardinal Gibbons, *The Faith of Our Fathers,* tenth edition, 1879, p. 108, available at https://1ref.us/234, accessed Sept. 22, 2022)

Here are also some **Protestant churches'** statements about the *Sabbath.*

Baptist

> There was and is a commandment to keep holy the Sabbath day, but that Sabbath day was not Sunday. It will be said, however, and with some show of triumph, that the Sabbath was transferred from the seventh to the first day of the week, with all its duties, privileges, and sanctions. Earnestly desiring information on this subject, which I have studied for many years, I ask, Where can the record of such a transaction be found? Not in the New Testament, absolutely not. There is no scriptural evidence of the change of the Sabbath institution from the seventh to the first day of the week. (Dr. Edward T. Hiscox, author of the *Hiscox Standard Baptist Manual,* in a paper read before a New York ministers' conference held Nov. 13, 1893, from a copy of the paper furnished by Dr. Hiscox)

Church of Christ

> Finally, we have the testimony of Christ on this subject. In Mark 2:27, he says: 'The Sabbath was made for man, and not man for the Sabbath.' From this passage it is evident that the Sabbath was made not merely for the Israelites, as Paley and Hengstenberg would have us believe, but for man ... that is, for the race. Hence we conclude that the Sabbath

was sanctified from the beginning, and that it was given to Adam, even in Eden, as one of those primeval institutions that God ordained for the happiness of all men. (Robert Milligan, *Scheme of Redemption*, St. Louis, The Bethany Press, 1962, p. 165)

Congregationalist

The Christian Sabbath [Sunday] is not in the Scriptures, and was not by the primitive church called *the Sabbath*. (Timothy Dwight, *Theology*, vol. 4, 1818, p. 49, available at https://1ref.us/236, accessed Sept. 22, 2022)

Episcopal

Sunday (*Dies Solis*, of the Roman calendar, "day of the sun," because dedicated to the sun), the first day of the week, was adopted by the early Christians as a day of worship. ... No regulations for its observance are laid down in the New Testament, nor, indeed, is its observance even enjoined ... ("Sunday," *A Religious Encyclopedia*, vol. 3, Philip Schaff, editor, New York, Funk and Wagnalls, 1882, p. 2259)

Lutheran

The observance of the Lord's day [Sunday] is founded not on any command of God, but on the authority of the church. (Augsburg Confession of Faith, quoted in Cox's *Sabbath Manual*, part 2, chap. 1, section 10)

Methodist

Take the matter of Sunday. There are indications in the New Testament as to how the church came to keep the first day of the week as its day of worship, but there is no passage telling Christians to keep that day, or to transfer the Jewish Sabbath to that day. (Harris Franklin Rall, *Christian Advocate*, July 2, 1942)

Moody Bible Institute

The Sabbath was binding in Eden, and it has been in force ever since. This fourth commandment begins with the word "remember," showing that the sabbath already existed when God wrote the law on the tables of stone at Sinai. How can men claim that this one commandment has been done away with when they will admit that the other nine are still binding? (D. L. Moody, *Weighed and Wanting*, 1898, p. 47, available at https://1ref.us/235, accessed Sept. 22, 2022)

Presbyterian

> Until, therefore, it can be shown that the whole moral law has been repealed, the Sabbath will stand. ... The teaching of Christ confirms the perpetuity of the Sabbath. (T. C. Blake, D.D., *Theology Condensed,* 1882, pp. 474, 475)

Pentecostal

> "Why do we worship on Sunday? Doesn't the Bible teach us that Saturday should be the Lord's Day?" ... Apparently we will have to seek the answer from some other source than the New Testament. (David A. Womack, "Is Sunday the Lord's Day?" *The Pentecostal Evangel,* Aug. 9, 1959, No. 2361, p. 3)

Presbyterian

> Sunday was a name given by the heathens to the first day of the week, because it was the day on which they worshipped the sun. ... The seventh day was blessed and hallowed by God himself, and ... He requires His creatures to keep it holy to Him. This commandment is of universal and perpetual obligation. (John Eadie, *A Biblical Cyclopedia,* 1872 ed., p. 561)

This is why Satan did not want you to study anything about the **mark of the beast.** It is because he does not want you to learn that God's people actually keep His created *holy Sabbath day.* He wants people to keep Sunday, so that, at the end of time, those who have the mark of the beast (**Sunday worship**) will be separated from God.

This is the first reason I call this book, *"Truth Will Make Us Free!"*

And God actually tells us this in **His Words:**

And ye shall know the *truth*, and the *truth* shall make you **free.** (John 8:32)

Chapter 7

The Truth about Hell

There is one other erroneous teaching that Satan created. It is about what happens when someone dies. Does man have an immortal soul? The King James Version of the Bible uses the word **"soul"** 1600 times, but *never once* does it use the term, **"*immortal* soul."**

The Greek word for "soul" is simply *psūche,* which generally means "breath."

The Hebrew word for soul is simply *nephesh,* which properly means "a breathing creature."

Let us begin our study by looking at the most common-sense text about *immortality* and who actually has it. It is found in 1 Timothy 6:16 and is about Jesus Christ Himself.

> *He alone is immortal; he lives in the light that no one can approach.*

Who **only** hath ***immortality*** [speaking of Jesus], dwelling in the light which no man can approach unto; whom no man hath seen, nor can see: to whom be honour and power everlasting. Amen. (1 Tim. 6:16)

The Greek word used in this text for immortality is *aphtharsia,* which means "unending existence." According to 1 Timothy 6:16, only God has "unending existence," or immortality. Let's look at the same verse in a more modern version.

> ***He* alone *is immortal;*** he lives in the light that no one can approach. No one has ever seen him; no one can ever see him. To him be honor and eternal power! Amen. (1 Tim. 6:16, GNT)

Now let us look at what Paul says about **man** and ***immortality.*** The second chapter of Romans discusses God's judgment of man. So, what Paul is talking about is who will be taken to heaven when Christ returns, that is, at the Second Coming.

> To them who by patient continuance in well doing *seek* for glory and honour and *immortality,* eternal life. (Rom. 2:7)

Paul tells us in Romans 2:7, that we don't possess **immortality,** but we *seek* it through Jesus Christ who died for our sins. We then get immortality when He returns to take us to heaven. Here's the same verse in a more modern version.

> Some people keep on doing good, and *seek* glory, honor, and *immortal* life; to them God will give eternal life. (Rom. 2:7, GNT)

Paul is explaining that Jesus wants to give us eternal life which means we do not have it now.

> For this corruptible must put on incorruption, and this *mortal* must put on *immortality.* (1 Cor. 15:53)

This verse tells us that we put on **immortality** at the Second Coming, which means we do not have it now. Again, let's look at the same verse in a more modern version.

> For what is mortal must be changed into what is immortal; what will die must be changed into what cannot die. (1 Cor. 15:53, GNT)

If you want to know the *trut* about what was written in the Bible in the Hebrew and Greek language and then translated into English, then you must go to Strong's Concordance to get the actual words. Strong assigned a number to every word written in the Old and New Testament Scriptures. Each Strong's numbers links a biblical word in Hebrew or Greek, in the original manuscripts, to the meaning in English of the Hebrew or Greek words.

When we study the Bible, Strong's numbers help us to achieve the following:

1. To understand the author's intended meaning of a word.
2. To easily find Bible words in their proper context.
3. To compare different usages of the same word.
4. The English language is complex, and a single word can have several different meanings. Strong's Concordance shows us which of those meanings is correct.

So, let us take a minute to look at the word "*soul*" itself using Strong's numbers.

Strong's number for the Hebrew word "soul" is *H5315*. The Hebrew word that Moses used, numbered H5315, is **nephesh.**

Here is the description of the **Hebrew** word **Nephesh**.

> **Nephesh H5315**
>
> From H5315; **properly a breathing creature,** that is, animal or (abstractly) vitality; used very widely in a literal, accommodated or figurative sense (bodily or mental): - any, appetite, beast, body, breath, creature, X dead (-ly), desire, X [dis-] contented, X fish, ghost, + greedy, he, heart (-y), (hath, X jeopardy of) life (X in jeopardy), lust, man, me, mind, mortality, one, own, person, pleasure, (her-, him-, my-, thy-) self, them (your) -selves, + slay, soul, + tablet, they, thing, (X she) will, X would have it.

So, the English word "soul" means basically a **"breathing creature."** The very first text in the Bible that uses the English word **"soul"** is found in **Genesis 2:7**. Here is the verse in the KJV:

> And the LORD God formed man of the dust of the ground, and breathed into his nostrils the breath of life; and man became a living soul [H5315 nephesh].

Now, here is the same text using Strong's numbers in a version known as **KJV+**. It links to the Hebrew word behind each English word using Strong's numbers.

> **Genesis 2:7+**
>
> And the LORD [**H3068**] God [**H430**] formed [**H3335**] man [**H120**] of the dust [**H6083**] of [**H4480**] the ground [**H127**], and breathed [**H5301**] into his nostrils [**H639**] the breath [**H5397**] of life [**H2416**]; and man [**H120**] became [**H1961**] a living [**H2416**] soul [**H5315**].

If you look up **Strong's number H5315,** you can find the author's *intended* meaning. Now I would like to share with you some other verses in which Moses used the word *nephesh (H5315).*

> **Genesis 1:20+**
>
> And God [**H430**] said [**H559**], Let the waters [**H4325**] bring forth abundantly [**H8317**] the moving creature [**H8318**] that hath life [**H5315**] [H2416], and fowl [**H5775**] that may fly [**H5774**] above [**H5921**] the earth [**H776**] in [**H5921**] the open [**H6440**] firmament [**H7549**] of heaven [**H8064**].

Here Moses uses the same word, translated *"soul"* in Genesis 2:7, for fish and birds.

Genesis 1:20

And God said, Let the waters bring forth abundantly the moving creature *that hath life [H5315 nephesh]*, and fowl that may fly above the earth in the open firmament of heaven.

For some reason, the Hebrew word *nephesh* was not translated as **"soul"** in this verse but as **"that hath life."**

Here is another verse that uses **nephesh (H5315).**

Genesis 1:21+

And God [**H430**] created [**H1254**] great [**H1419**] whales [**H8577**], and every [**H3605**] living [**H2416**] *creature [H5315]* that moveth, [**H7430**] which [**H834**] the waters [**H4325**] brought forth abundantly [**H8317**], after their kind [**H4327**], and every [**H3605**] winged [**H3671**] fowl [**H5775**] after his kind [**H4327**]: and God [**H430**] saw [**H7200**] that [**H3588**] it was good. [**H2896**].

In this verse, Moses uses the same word, translated *"soul"* in Genesis 2:7, for all living creatures which the waters brought forth.

Genesis 1:21

And God created great whales, and every living *creature [H5315 nephesh]* that moveth, which the waters brought forth abundantly, after their kind, and every winged fowl after his kind: and God saw that it was good.

The last verse I want to share with you is **Genesis 1:24.**

Genesis 1:24+

And God [**H430**] said [**H559**], Let the earth [**H776**] bring forth [**H3318**] the living [**H2416**] creature [**H5315** nephesh] after his kind [**H4327**], cattle, [**H929**], and creeping thing, [**H7431**] and beast [**H2416**] of the earth [**H776**] after his kind [**H4327**]: and it was [**H1961**] so [**H3651**].

Here Moses uses the same word, translated *"soul"* in Genesis 2:7, for cattle and all the animals God created on the earth.

Genesis 1:24

And God said, Let the earth bring forth the living *creature [H5315 nephesh]* after his kind, cattle, and creeping thing, and beast of the earth after his kind: and it was so.

So, according to Moses, every fish, bird, and animal created by God—including man—is nothing other than a ***breathing creature!*** So, this definition destroys the idea that there is such a thing as what Christians refer to as an **"*immortal soul.*"**

> **Where did the idea of an immortal soul that burns for eternity come from?**

Following is a verse that says that iniquity was already taking place while the Bible was being written for us.

> For the mystery of iniquity ***doth already work:*** only he who now letteth will let, until he be taken out of the way. (2 Thess. 2:7)

A modern version says, "The Mysterious Wickedness is already at work." Paul taught that a falling away from the truth would come so the man of sin could be revealed, a power already at work in his day. More than three hundred years before Paul, the idea of an immortal soul was being developed.

Plato 424–347 BC

"Plato's main argument for the ***immortality of the soul*** is found in his Phaedo. Following contemporary Greek religious belief and Socrates' assumption that everything is involved in an eternal cyclical process, **Plato** naturally understands immortality (and pre-existence) of the soul in terms of **reincarnation.** Plato draws an analogy with sleep. Sleep comes after being awake and being awake comes after sleep. Likewise, just as death comes from life so must death return to life again" ("Plato's Immortality of the Soul," Stafford Grammar School Scandalon, https://1ref.us/22g, accessed Sept. 22, 2022).

During the last half of the second century the center of intellectualism and contemporary thinking in the Christian world was in Alexandria, Egypt. It was there, through the writings of **Athenagoras** (A.D. 127–190), that we find the ***first mention of man having an immortal soul.***

Athenagoras was trained in ***pagan Greek learning and the philosophy of Plato*** before he became a Christian. Apparently becoming a Christian did not invalidate his former views since he was the ***first ecclesiastical writer to publicly embrace the immortality of the soul.*** Without referencing **Scripture**, Athenagoras presented his views directly from Plato's philosophy. His theology **"*is strongly tinged with Platonism*"** ("Athenagoras," *Encyclopedia Britannica*, 11th edition, p. 831).

"**Athenagoras** frequently combined the beliefs of the Greek poets and philosophers, particularly Plato, with the doctrines of Christianity" (*Encyclopedia Americana*, volume 2, 2001, p. 605).

According to professor of historical theology Dr. LeRoy Froom, **Athenagoras'** "main premise was that God's purpose in creating man was that he should live—that the divine purpose of man's existence is existence itself. And God's purpose, he contended, cannot be defeated. It must be accomplished. It is therefore impossible for man to cease to exist" (Dr. LeRoy E. Froom, *The Conditionalist Faith of our Fathers,* Washington, D.C.: Review and Herald Publishing Assoc., 1965], vol. 1, p. 931).

The conclusion of this argument was **"*compulsory immortality*"** for all. With regard to the wicked, Athenagoras reasoned, they must live forever in eternal misery; and they must exist eternally because the primary reason God made man is for the purpose of living.

While it was **Athenagoras** who launched publicly the concept of an *immortal soul,* it was a younger contemporary of his, **Tertullian of Carthage** (A.D. 160–240), who pursued and amplified it. He was the first of the church fathers to write in Latin, soon to be the official language of the medieval church. Prior to his conversion at the age of 40, Tertullian received a Greco-Roman education in Rome.

According to Froom, **"*it was Tertullian who first affirmed that the torments of the lost will be coequal and coexistent with the happiness of the saved*"** (Froom, p. 950).

Tertullian's propositions needed other modifications: "He [Tertullian] confessedly altered the sense of Scripture and the meaning of words, ***so as to interpret 'death' as eternal misery, and 'destruction' and 'consume' as pain and anguish. 'Hell' became perpetually dying, but never dead***" (Froom, p. 951).

Without hesitation, Tertullian referred directly to Plato in his writings. Plato's primary theme, **"*every soul is immortal,*"** became Tertullian's unwavering platform (Tertullian, "On the Resurrection," *Ante-Nicene Fathers,* chap. 3, p. 547).

The church fathers who followed suit by including Tertullian's propositions in their public preaching and writing were **Minucius Felix, Cyprian of Carthage, Ambrose of Milan, John Chrysostom, and Jerome** (the translator of the Bible into the Latin Vulgate).

Did they follow blindly? Were these leaders naive? Dr. Froom observes: "It is to be particularly noted that all Christian Fathers who use this 'immortal soul' phrase or thought were not only familiar with but likewise in accord with this position in the writing of Plato. And it is also to be observed that none of such early Christian writers ever sought for support for this doctrine by primary appeal to Scripture, but had recourse instead to arguments similar to those used by Plato" (Froom, p. 954).

It is my conclusion that, if one is *looking for truth* and believes that the Word of God is the only source of truth, then the idea of man's immortal soul *and, by extension, the ever-burning of his body in hell are impossible.*

There is no scriptural foundation for man's **immortal soul** except the immortality he receives at Jesus' second coming with **his new life on the earth made new.**

> And I saw *a new heaven* and *a new earth:* for the first heaven and the first earth were passed away; and there was no more sea. ² And I John saw the holy city, New Jerusalem, coming down from God out of heaven, prepared as a bride adorned for her husband. ³ And I heard a great voice out of heaven saying, Behold, the tabernacle of God is with men, and he will dwell with them, and they shall be his people, and **God himself shall be with them,** and be their God.
>
> ⁴ And God shall wipe away all tears from their eyes; and there shall be no more death, neither sorrow, nor crying, neither shall there be any more pain: for the former things are passed away. ⁵ And he that sat upon the throne said, Behold, I make all things new. And he said unto me, Write: for these words are true and faithful. ⁶ And he said unto me, It is done. I am Alpha and Omega, the beginning and the end. I will give unto him that is athirst of the fountain of the water of life freely. ⁷ He that overcometh shall inherit all things; and I will be his God, and he shall be my son. (Rev. 21:1–7)

So, the answer to the question, **"Does man have an immortal soul?"** is, according to God's Holy Word, a decided *NO!*

However, we will receive an immortal soul (breathing life) after we are taken to heaven after Jesus' second coming.

Chapter 8

Eternal Burning Hell – Fact or Fiction?

Without a doubt, the following is one of the most popular verses in the Bible:

> For God so *loved* the world, that he gave his only begotten Son, that whosoever believeth in him should not perish, but have everlasting life. (John 3:16)

This statement tells us that God loves all of us, and that is why He gave us Jesus Christ to save us from our sins. Now, here are three more verses about *love.*

> He that loveth not knoweth not God; for **God is love.** (1 John 4:8)

> But as it is written, Eye hath not seen, nor ear heard, neither have entered into the heart of man, **the things which God hath prepared for them that love him.** (1 Cor. 2:9)

> The LORD hath appeared of old unto me, saying, Yea, I have loved thee with an ***everlasting love:*** therefore, ***with lovingkindness have I drawn thee.*** (Jer. 31:3)

These texts tell us that **God is love!**

If God is love, then why do some people portray Him as a despicable and heartless tyrant who will take His very own children and torture them without mercy or relief throughout all eternity?

It seems incredible that, while society locks **child abusers** in prison, so many people are willing to hold God guilty of the most horrible case of child abuse ever perpetrated—lighting His own children on fire and then watching them burn in hell forever!

Although I do believe God will destroy the wicked in hell, I don't believe He will torture them with fire for all eternity, and here is why. Consider first what Isaiah says about God's work of punishing.

> For the LORD shall rise up as in mount Perazim, he shall be wroth as in the valley of Gibeon, that he may do his work, **his *strange* work;** and bring to pass his act, **his *strange* act.** (Isa. 28:21)

The Bible says that, when God destroys the wicked, it is a ***strange act.*** This is because God is *love,* and He does *not* want to destroy the wicked. Rather, He wants them to repent so He can save them. But if they do not repent, then, due to the just sentence that "*wages of sin is death,*" they will ave to be destroyed.

> Say unto them, As I live, saith the Lord GOD, ***I have no pleasure in the death of the wicked;*** but that the wicked turn from his way and live: turn ye, turn ye from your evil ways; for why will ye *die,* O house of Israel? (Ezek. 33:11)

> *As I live, saith the Lord GOD, I have no pleasure in the death of the wicked.*

What does God mean by "the ***death*** of the wicked"? If He plans on torturing people for eternity, then why didn't He say, "I have no pleasure in torturing the wicked for eternity?" What does God mean by "death"?

> These things said he: and after that he saith unto them, Our friend Lazarus ***sleepeth;*** but I go, that I may awake him out of sleep. (John 11:11)

The Greek word for "sleepeth" is *koimao,* which means "put to sleep, or deceased."

Jesus compares death to ***sleep*** over 50 times in Scripture. Then too He speaks of the resurrection—actually of two resurrections.

> *If He plans on torturing people for eternity, then why didn't He say, "I have no pleasure in torturing the wicked for eternity?"*

> Marvel not at this: for the hour is coming, in the which all that are **in the graves** shall hear his voice, ⁹ And shall come forth; they that have done good, unto the ***resurrection of life;*** and they that have done evil, unto the ***resurrection of damnation.*** (John 5:28, 29)

So, there are two resurrections—one for those who will live eternally with God and one for those who will be burned in hell. If the dead will have gone directly to heaven or hell immediately when they died, then how would they *hear* God's call from the grave? God's Word does not say that a person's spirit in heaven or hell hears God's voice and then rejoins the person's body in the grave to come forth. And there is something else about the following verse, which we have already read.

> And the LORD God formed man of the dust of the ground, and breathed into his nostrils the breath of life; and man became a living ***soul.*** (Gen. 2:7)

As we said before, the Hebrew word for "soul" is *nephesh*—a breathing creature—and the Greek the word for "soul" is *psūche*, or breath. The verse doesn't say that God put a soul *in* man, it says that man simply *became* a living soul when the two elements were combined and the man could breathe. So, with that in mind, here is the other thought: Genesis 2:7 simply states what the equation below represents.

Dust + the breath of God = a soul (a breathing creature).

When we die, what actually happens is that we simply lose our ***breath, or spirit,*** and our ***dust*** returns to the ground. Here is the Bible verse that says that.

> Then shall the dust return to the earth as it was: and the ***spirit*** shall return unto God who gave it. (Eccl. 12:7)

(The word for ***"spirit"*** in Hebrew is *ruach*, which means "wind" or "breath." The word for ***"spirit"*** in Greek is *pneuma,* which means "wind" or "breeze.") If you reverse the equation, it then looks like this.

Soul - the breath of God = dust.

So, the Bible says that, when we die, it is our breath that goes back to God while our body becomes dust here on our earth.

An example of something that, if destroyed, would be ***similar*** to what the Bible says happens to us when we die is the following:

A light bulb + electricity = light.

Light - electricity = (a dark) light bulb.

If we take away the electricity from the light bulb, all we have is a dead or darkened bulb. Consider David's admonition:

> Put not your trust in princes, nor in the son of man, in whom there is no help. ⁴ His **breath** goeth forth, he returneth to his earth; in that very day **his thoughts perish.** (Ps. 146:3, 4)

According to David, people have **no thoughts** after they die. Or, putting it another way, he says:

> The dead praise not the LORD, neither any that go down into silence. (Ps. 115:17)

The Bible tells us that, when we go to heaven, **we will sing** and praise God. Yet, since David says the dead do not praise God, it must mean that we do not go immediately to heaven when we die. Peter affirms this truth, talking about David himself.

> For David is **not ascended** into the heavens: but he saith himself, The LORD said unto my Lord, Sit thou on my right hand. (Acts 2:34)

If anyone should be in heaven, surely it would be David, a man after God's own heart. The only explanation that he is not is that he is simply sleeping in the grave awaiting Christ's return. David adds:

> For in death there is **no remembrance** of thee: in the grave who shall give thee thanks? (Ps. 6:5)

If there is **no remembrance** of Christ in the grave, then when we die, we must simply be sleeping.

> For the living know that they shall die: but the dead **know not any thing,** neither have they any more a reward; for the memory of them is forgotten. ⁶ Also, their love, and their hatred, and their envy, is now **perished;** neither have they any more a portion forever in anything that is done under the sun. (Eccl. 9:5, 6)

If the dead know nothing in the grave, then they cannot be going to heaven or hell when they die.

> Whatsoever thy hand findeth to do, do it with thy might; for there is no work, nor device, nor knowledge, nor wisdom, in the grave, whither thou goest. (Eccl. 9:10)

Here again it says that, when we die, **we know nothing.**

> And fear not them which kill the body, but are not able to kill the **soul:** but rather fear him which is able to destroy both **soul** and body in hell. (Matt. 10:28)

Once again the word **"soul" means breath.** Apparently, we are to fear Him who can take away our breath.

God has been extremely patient with His people.

> The Lord is not slack concerning his promise, as some men count slackness; but is longsuffering to us-ward, not willing that any should **perish,** but that all should come to repentance. (2 Peter 3:9)

The Greek word here for "perish" is *apollumi,* which means "to destroy fully." Can we not see that, if sinners are **destroyed fully**, it means that they cannot burn forever in hell?

> For God so loved the world, that he gave his only begotten Son, that whosoever believeth in him should not **perish,** but have everlasting life. (John 3:16)

The same Greek word for "perish" is used here—*apollumi.* Again it means "to **destroy fully.**" If a person is destroyed fully, then that does not sound like he or she can be living in torment for eternity. In this context is another biblical statement:

> For our God *is* a **consuming** fire. (Heb. 12:29)

The Greek word for "consuming" is *katanaliskō,* which means "to consume utterly." A person can't be utterly **consumed** but then burn forever. That's impossible. This leads us to another statement from the Psalms.

> For yet a little while, and the wicked **shall not be:** yea, thou shalt diligently consider his place, and it shall not be. (Ps. 37:10)

The Hebrew term for "shall not be" uses the word *ayin,* which means **exist.** In other words, the wicked will not exist. How can a person not exist but burn in hell for eternity?

> But the wicked shall **perish,** and the enemies of the LORD *shall be* as the fat of lambs: they shall **consume;** into smoke shall they consume away. (Ps. 37:20)

The Hebrew word for "perish" here is *kalah,* which means "**be finished.**" How can you turn into smoke if you are burning in hell forever? Smoke is the result of something being consumed.

> And they [*the wicked*] went up on the breadth of the earth, and compassed the camp of the saints about, and the beloved city [*New*

> *Jerusalem*]: and fire came down from God out of heaven, and ***devoured*** them. (Rev. 20:9)

The Greek word for "devoured" here is *katesthiō*, which means **"to devour."** If something is ***devoured***, it cannot last forever. Consider the fate of those who rebel against God.

> For as ye have drunk upon my holy mountain, *so* shall all the **heathen** drink continually, yea, they shall drink, and they shall swallow down, and they shall ***be as though they had not been.*** (Obadiah 1:16)

The Hebrew phrase for "be as though they had not been" is *lo lo loh*, which means that they would be as if they **"never existed."** Someone who becomes as if he ***never existed*** must not be burning eternally. The next verse shows how completely the destruction takes place.

> Looking for and hasting unto the coming of the day of God, wherein the heavens being on fire shall be ***dissolved,*** and the elements shall melt with fervent heat? [13] Nevertheless we, according to his promise, look for new heavens and a new earth, wherein dwelleth righteousness. (2 Peter 3:12, 13)

The Greek word here for "dissolved" is *lūo*, which means **"*destroyed.*"** How could God make a new earth with people continually burning on it? David makes this thought plain.

> I have seen **the wicked** in great power, and spreading himself like a green bay tree. Yet he passed away, **and, lo, he was not:** yea, I sought him, **but he could not be found.** Mark the perfect man, and behold the upright: for the end of that man is peace. But the transgressors shall be ***destroyed*** together: the end of the wicked shall be cut off. But the salvation of the righteous is of the LORD: he is their strength in the time of trouble. And the LORD shall help them, and deliver them: he shall deliver them from the wicked, and save them, because they trust in him. (Ps. 37:35–40)

The Hebrew word here for "destroyed," *shamad*, simply means **"*destroyed.*"** People who are destroyed cannot be alive and still burning. No, God makes it plain what will happen to them.

> For, behold, the day cometh, that shall ***burn*** as an oven; and all the proud, yea, and all that do wickedly, **shall be stubble:** and the day that cometh shall ***burn them up,*** saith the LORD of hosts, that it shall leave

> them neither root nor branch. ² But unto you that fear my name shall the Sun of righteousness arise with healing in his wings; and ye shall go forth, and grow up as calves of the stall. ³ And ye shall tread down the wicked; for they shall be **ashes under the soles of your feet** in the day that I shall do this, saith the LORD of hosts. (Malachi 4:1–3)

If the wicked are burned up into ashes that we will walk on, then they cannot burn forever while we are walking on them! But what about the description in Revelation?

> And the devil that deceived them was cast into the lake of fire and brimstone, where the beast and the false prophet are, and shall be tormented day and night ***for ever and ever.*** (Rev. 20:10)

The Greek word for the phrase "for ever and ever" is *aion,* which refers to **"*an age.*"** So, the original language claims that **Satan** will burn for **an age**. What is an age? We do not know what an age is, but its use proves from the original language that Satan will not burn without end in hell.

Common sense tells us that if hell burns forever **"on the breadth of the earth,"** it would be impossible for God to create a new earth. And if God kept Satan alive to endure an eternal burning, He would fail in His mission to rid the world of sin. Instead, He would perpetuate it. To understand this, we must look at the literal translation from the Greek language of an **"age."** I for one cannot determine the length of an "age" from the word itself, so I will have to let other scriptures speak about the outcome of Satan's punishment. Consider the following.

Does Satan burn forever?

> By the multitude of thy merchandise they have filled the midst of thee with violence, and thou hast sinned: therefore I will cast thee as profane out of the mountain of God: and I will ***destroy*** thee, O covering cherub, from the midst of the stones of fire. ¹⁷ Thine heart was lifted up because of thy beauty; thou hast corrupted thy wisdom by reason of thy brightness: I will cast thee to the ground; I will lay thee before kings, that they may behold thee. ¹⁸ Thou hast defiled thy sanctuaries by the multitude of thine iniquities, by the iniquity of thy traffick; therefore will I bring forth a fire from the midst of thee, it shall ***devour*** thee, and ***I will bring thee to ashes upon the earth*** in the sight of all them that behold thee. ¹⁹ All they that know thee among the people shall be astonished at thee: thou shalt be a terror, and ***never shalt thou be any more.*** (Ezek. 28:16–18)

The Hebrew word here for "destroy" is *abad,* which means **"to perish."** The Hebrew word here for "devour" is *akal,* or **"consume."** Here it is clear that **Satan becomes ashes** on the earth exactly as the wicked do. God also says of Satan, **"Never shalt thou be any more."** I can only conclude that an "age" is not for all eternity without end. The fire must go out after it does its work. Otherwise, Satan would not become ashes under our feet and would still be living in hell fire. So, Satan will burn for a period of time described as an **"age,"** which we do not know how long it will be.

The biblical meaning of the word "forever"

In other references in Scripture, the term **"forever"** is used in conjunction with an event that cannot possibly go on for eternity without end. For instance, Hannah pledged to God that she would take her infant son Samuel to serve in the temple at Shiloh, where he would abide **"forever"** (1 Samuel 1:22).

No student of the Bible would take this to mean that he would remain in that temple for as long as time should last. Hannah herself interpreted the statement as meaning that Samuel would serve in the temple for **"as long as he liveth"** (verse 28).

Another example of "forever" is in Jonah's statement that he was in the belly of the fish **"forever"** (Jonah 2:6). Yet we know that he endured his eerie journey beneath the sea for just **"three days and three nights"** (Jonah 1:17). Are there other examples? Here's one in Exodus.

> Then his master shall bring him unto the judges; he shall also bring him to the door, or unto the door post; and his master shall bore his ear through with an aul; and he shall serve him **forever.** (Exod. 21:6)

There are no Bible slaves still living today serving their masters.

What about the statement in Revelation about the smoke of torment?

> And the *smoke* of their torment **ascendeth up** for *ever and ever:* and they have no rest day nor night, who worship the beast and his image, and whosoever receiveth the mark of his name. (ReZv. 14:11)

Again, the word translated "for ever and ever" means an **"age."** Also, notice that it is the smoke that ascends up for an "age."

So what does it mean biblically? More than fifty times the Bible uses **"for ever"** to mean "for as long as time lasts in that specific case." Even today we use the term to describe a downpour or a sweltering hot summer afternoon (or a sermon!) as going on **"forever."** Here's another biblical phrase we need to understand—"everlasting fire."

> Then shall he say also unto them on the left hand, Depart from me, ye cursed, into ***everlasting fire,*** prepared for the devil and his angels. (Matt. 25:41)

The Greek word for "everlasting" in "*everlasting* fire" is *aionios,* or ***perpetual.*** If so many scriptures tell us that the wicked will be "burned up," or nonexistent, then this can only mean that the *fire* is everlasting but not the punishing. In other words, its effects are what is everlasting.

> Even as Sodom and Gomorrah, and the cities about them in like manner, giving themselves over to fornication, and going after strange flesh, are set forth for an example, suffering the vengeance of ***eternal fire.*** (Jude 1:7)

The Greek word for "eternal" in "eternal fire" is *aionios,* or ***perpetual.*** Are Sodom and Gomorrah still burning today? The fire that destroyed Sodom and Gomorrah is the same as the fire of hell, it only lasts until it finishes its work.

> I indeed baptize you with water unto repentance: but he that cometh after me is mightier than I, whose shoes I am not worthy to bear: he shall baptize you with the Holy Ghost, and with fire: [12] Whose fan is in his hand, and he will thoroughly purge his floor, and gather his wheat into the garner; but he will **burn up** the chaff with ***unquenchable fire.*** (Matt. 3:11, 12)

The Greek word for the phrase "burn up" is *asbestos,* which means **"*not to be extinguished.*"** The fire cannot be put out until it finishes its work. But once the material is burned up, then the fire can quit.

> And these shall go away into **everlasting punishment**: but the righteous into life eternal. (Matt. 25:46)

It is the punishment that is everlasting, not the punishing—the results, not the process.

So what about the use of "hell" in Second Peter?

> For if God spared not the angels that sinned, but cast *them* down to **hell,** and delivered *them* into chains of darkness, to be **reserved** unto judgment. (2 Peter 2:4)

The Greek word here for "hell" is *tartaroo,* a word used to describe ***the deepest abyss of hades.*** See Revelation 20:1 where it says that Satan will be chained to the bottomless pit or deep abyss for 1000 years. "Reserved" actually means that hell is for a time in the future and not burning right now. There is another statement about the fire that destroyed Sodom and Gomorrah.

> And turning the cities of Sodom and Gomorrah **into ashes** condemned *them* with an overthrow, making *them* an ensample unto those that after should live ungodly; ⁹ The Lord knoweth how to deliver the godly out of temptations, and to reserve the unjust unto **the day of judgment to be punished.** (2 Peter 2:6, 9)

If hell is said to be unto a day of judgment, then it is not burning now but will burn in the future. So, if hell isn't burning now, and it doesn't burn for eternity, then exactly what, where, and when does it burn? A passage in Revelation gives the answer.

> And I saw an angel come down from heaven, having the key of the bottomless pit and a great chain in his hand. ² And he laid hold on the dragon, that old serpent, which is the Devil, and Satan, and bound him a **thousand years,** ³ And cast him into the bottomless pit, and shut him up, and set a seal upon him, that he should deceive the nations no more, till the **thousand years** should be fulfilled: and after that he must be loosed a little season. ⁴ And I saw thrones, and they [the righteous] sat upon them, and judgment was given unto them: and I saw the souls of them that were beheaded for the witness of Jesus, and for the word of God, and which had not worshipped the beast, neither his image, neither had received his mark upon their foreheads, or in their hands; **and they lived and reigned with Christ a thousand years.** ⁵ But the rest of the dead lived not again until the **thousand years** were finished. This is the **first resurrection.** ⁶ Blessed and holy is he that hath part in the first resurrection: on such the second **death hath** no power, but they shall be priests of God and of Christ, and shall reign with him a **thousand years.** ⁷ And when the **thousand years** are expired, Satan shall be loosed out of his prison, ⁸ And shall go out to deceive the nations which are in the four quarters of the earth, Gog and Magog, to gather them together to battle: the number of whom is as the sand of the sea. ⁹ And they went up on the breadth of the earth, and compassed the camp of the saints about, and the beloved city: **and fire came down from God out of heaven, and devoured them.** ¹⁰ **And the devil that deceived them was cast into the lake of fire and brimstone,** where the beast and the false prophet are, and shall be tormented day and night *for ever and ever* [**Greek, *aion,* "an age"**]. ¹¹ And I saw a great white throne, and him that sat on it, from whose face the earth and

> the heaven fled away; and ***there was found no place for them.*** ¹² And I saw the dead, small and great, stand before God; and the books were opened: and another book was opened, which is the book of life: and the dead were judged out of those things which were written in the books, according to their works. ¹³ And the sea gave up the dead which were in it; and death and hell [***grave***] delivered up the dead which were in them: and they were judged every man according to their works. ¹⁴ ***And death and hell were cast into the lake of fire.*** This is the ***second death.*** ¹⁵ And whosoever was not found written in the book of life was cast into the lake of fire. (Rev. 20:1–15)

At the end of this earth's history, Jesus will take His saints to heaven for one thousand years. Then, after the one thousand years are complete, they will return to this earth with Jesus, as the New Jerusalem also descends upon the earth. It is after those one thousand years that hell fire destroys Satan and the wicked, and, after they are turned into ashes, God will create a new earth. Then Jesus will dwell with the redeemed for eternity ***upon the ashes*** of the wicked.

What Revelation describes is what will happen at the end of this world *after* hell destroys the wicked (which is a ***second death)*** and ***Satan*** is also destroyed. It is Satan's lie that the wicked head to hell immediately when they die the "first death" and that they burn forever. It is a lie because there is actually a second death, according to God's Word, proving that burning in hell forever without end is a ***satanic lie.*** So what is the truth?

> And I saw a new heaven and a new earth: for the first heaven and the first earth were passed away; and there was no more sea. ² And I John saw the holy city, New Jerusalem, coming down from God out of heaven, prepared as a bride adorned for her husband. ³ And I heard a great voice out of heaven saying***, behold, the tabernacle of God is with men,*** and he will dwell with them, and they shall be his people, and God himself shall be with them, and be their God. ⁴ And God shall wipe away all tears from their eyes; and there shall be no more death, neither sorrow, nor crying, neither shall there be any more pain: for the ***former things are passed away.*** ⁵ And he that sat upon the throne said, Behold, I make all things new. And he said unto me, Write: for these words are true and faithful. … ⁸ But the fearful, and unbelieving, and the abominable, and murderers, and whoremongers, and sorcerers, and idolaters, and all liars, shall have their part in the lake which burneth with fire and brimstone: which is ***the second death.*** (Rev. 21:1–5, 8)

Now you know the truth.

> And ye shall know the truth, and the truth shall make you free. (John 8:32)

> You will know the truth, and the truth will set you free. (John 8:32, GNT)

> And you will have knowledge of what is true, and that will make you free. (John 8:32, BBE)

TEACH Services, Inc.
P U B L I S H I N G

We invite you to view the complete
selection of titles we publish at:
www.TEACHServices.com

We encourage you to write us
with your thoughts about this,
or any other book we publish at:
info@TEACHServices.com

TEACH Services' titles may be purchased in
bulk quantities for educational, fund-raising,
business, or promotional use.
bulksales@TEACHServices.com

Finally, if you are interested in seeing
your own book in print, please contact us at:
publishing@TEACHServices.com
We are happy to review your manuscript at no charge.

www.ingramcontent.com/pod-product-compliance
Lightning Source LLC
Chambersburg PA
CBHW042133160426
43199CB00021B/2896